Mrs. Inchbald

Such Things Are

A Play in Five Acts

Mrs. Inchbald

Such Things Are
A Play in Five Acts

ISBN/EAN: 9783744661522

Printed in Europe, USA, Canada, Australia, Japan

Cover: Foto ©Thomas Meinert / pixelio.de

More available books at **www.hansebooks.com**

PLAY,

IN

FIVE ACTS

AS PERFORMED AT THE

THEATRE ROYAL, COVENT GARDEN,

Mrs. INCHBALD.

SECOND

Printed for G. G.

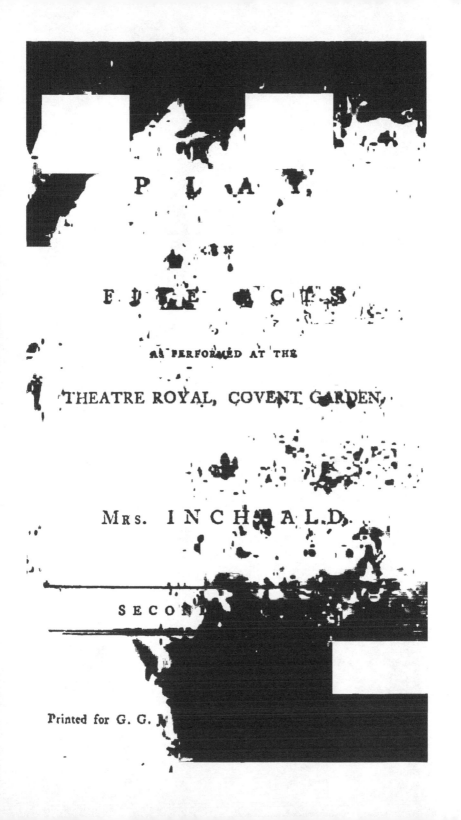

ADVERTISEMENT.

THE travels of an Englishman throughout Europe, and even in some parts of Asia, to soften the sorrows of the Prisoner, excited in the mind of the Author the subject of the following pages, which, formed into a dramatic story, have produced from the Theatre a profit far exeeeding the usual pecuniary advantages arising from a successful Comedy.

The uncertainty in what part of the East the hero of the present piece was (at the time it was written) dispensing his benevolence, caused the Writer, after many researches and objections, to fix the scene on the island of Sumatra, where the English settlement, the system of government, and every description of the manners of the people, reconcile the incidents of the Play to the strictest degree of probability.

P R O L O G U E,

Written by THOMAS VAUGHAN, Efq.

Spoken by Mr. HOLMAN.

HOW say you, critic Gods*, and you below †;
Are you all friends ?—or here—and there—a foe ?
Come to protect your *literary* trade,
Which Mrs. *Scribble* dares *again* invade—
But know you not—*in all* the fair ones do,
'Tis not to pleafe themfelves alone—but you.
Then who fo churlifh, or fo cynic grown,
Would wifh to change a *fimper* for a *frown* ?
Or who fo jealous of their own *dear* quill,
Would point the paragraph her fame to kill ?
Yet fuch there are, in this all-fcribbling town, ⎫
And men of letters too—of fome renown, ⎬
Who ficken at all merit but their own. ⎭
But fure 'twere more for Wit's—for Honour's fake,
To make the Drama's *race—the give and take.*

        [Looking round the houfe.
My hint I fee's approv'd—fo pray begin it,
And praife us—*roundly* for the *good things* in it,
Nor let feverity our faults expofe,
When godlike Homer's felf was known to doze.
 But of the piece—Methinks I hear you hint,
Some dozen lines or more fhould give the tint—
" Tell how *Sir John* with *Lady Betty*'s maid
" Is caught intriguing at a mafquerade ;
" Which Lady Betty, in a jealous fit,
" Refents by flirting with *Sir Ben*—the cit.
" Whofe *three*-feet fpoufe, to modifh follies bent,
" Miftakes a *fix*-feet Valet—for a Gent.

         " While

PROLOGUE.

" Whilſt Miſs, repugnant to her Guardian's plan,
" Elopes in Breeches with her fav'rite man."
Such are the *hints* we read in *Roſcius'* days,
By way of Prologue uſhered in *their* plays.
But *we*, like Miniſters and cautious ſpies,
In *ſecret meaſures* think—the merit lies.
Yet ſhall the Muſe thus far unveil the plot—
This play was *tragi-comically* got,
Thoſe ſympathetic ſorrows to impart
Which harmonize the feelings of the heart;
And may at leaſt this humble merit boaſt,
A ſtructure founded on fair *Fancy*'s coaſt.
With you it reſts that judgement to proclaim,
Which *in the world* muſt raiſe or ſink it's fame.
Yet ere her judges ſign their laſt report,
'Tis you [*to the boxes*] muſt recommend her to the Court;
Whoſe ſmiles, like *Cynthia*, in a winter's night,
Will cheer our wand'rer with a gleam of light.

＊ Galleries.   † Pit.

ACT I.

SCENE, *The Ifland of Sumatra, in Eaſt India.*

CHARACTERS.

MEN.

Sultan, - - - - - - -	Mr. Farren,
Lord Flint, - - - - - -	Mr. Davies,
Sir Luke Tremor, - - - -	Mr. Quick,
Mr. Twineall, - - - - -	Mr. Lewis,
Mr. Haſwell, - - - - -	Mr. Pope,
Elvirus, - - - - - -	Mr. Holman,
Mr. Meanright, - - - -	Mr. Macready,
Zedan, - - - - - - -	Mr. Fearon,
Firſt Keeper, - - - - -	Mr. Thompſon,
Second Keeper, - - - - -	Mr. Cubitt,
Firſt Priſoner, - - - - -	Mr. Helme,
Second Priſoner, - - - -	Mr. Gardener.
Guard, - - - - - - -	Mr. Blurton,
Meſſenger, - - - - - -	Mr. Ledger.

WOMEN.

Lady Tremor, - - - - -	Mrs. Mattocks,
Aurelia, - - - - - -	Miſs Wilkinſon,
Female Priſoner, - - - -	Mrs. Pope.

Time of Repreſentation, Twelve Hours.

4

SUCH THINGS ARE.

A PLAY.

IN FIVE ACTS.

A C T   I.

S C E N E I. *A Parlour at Sir* Luke Tremor's.

Enter Sir Luke, *followed by Lady* Tremor.

Sir Luke.

I TELL you, Madam, you are two and thirty.
Lady Tremor. I tell you, Sir, you are miſtaken.
Sir Luke. Why, did not you come over from England exactly ſixteen years ago?
Lady. Not ſo long.
Sir Luke. Have not we been married the tenth of next April ſixteen years?
Lady. Not ſo long.—
Sir Luke. Did you not come over the year of the great Eclipſe? anſwer me that.
Lady. I don't remember it.
Sir Luke. But I do—and ſhall remember it as long as I live—the firſt time I ſaw you, was in the garden of the Dutch Envoy; you were looking through a glaſs at the ſun—I immediately began to make love to you, and the whole affair was

B   ſettled

settled while the eclipse lasted—just one hour, eleven minutes, and three seconds.

Lady. But what is all this to my age?

Sir Luke. Because I know you were at that time near seventeen—and without one qualification except your youth—and not being a Mullatto.

Lady. Sir Luke, Sir Luke, this is not to be borne—

Sir Luke. Oh! yes—I forgot—you had two letters of recommendation, from two great families in England.

Lady. Letters of recommendation!

Sir Luke. Yes; your character——that, you know, is all the fortune we poor Englishmen, situated in India, expect with a wife who crosses the sea at the hazard of her life, to make us happy.

Lady. And what but our characters would you have us bring? Do you suppose any lady ever came to India, who brought along with her, friends, or fortune?

Sir Luke. No, my dear—and what is worse—she seldom leaves them behind, either.

Lady. No matter, Sir Luke—but if I delivered to you a good character——

Sir Luke. Yes, my dear you did—and if you were to ask me for it again, I can't say I could give it you.

Lady. How uncivil! how unlike are your manners to the manners of my Lord Flint.

Sir Luke. Ay —you are never so happy as when you have an opportunity of expressing your admiration of him—a disagreeable, nay, a very dangerous man—one is never sure of one's self in his presence—he carries every thing he hears to the ministers of our suspicious Sultan—and I feel my head shake whenever I am in his company.

Lady. How different does his Lordship appear to me—to me he is all *politesse*.

Sir

Sir Luke. *Politeſſe!* how fhou'd you under-derftand what is real *politeſſe?* You know your education was very much confined.——

Lady. And if it *was* confined——I beg, Sir Luke, you will one time or other ceafe thefe re-flections—you know they are what I can't bear! [*walks about in a paſſion.*] pray, does not his Lord-fhip continually affure me, I might be taken for a Countefs, were it not for a certain little groveling tofs I have caught with my head—and a certain little confined hitch in my walk? both which I learnt of *you*—learnt by looking fo much at *you.*——

Sir Luke. And now if you don't take care, by looking fo much at his Lordfhip, you may catch fome of his defects.

Lady. I know of very few he has.

Sir Luke. I know of many—befides thofe he affumes.——

Lady. Affumes ! !——

Sir Luke. Yes ; do you fuppofe he is as forget-ful as he pretends to be? no, no—but becaufe he is a favourite with the Sultan, and all our great men at court, he thinks it genteel or convenient to have no memory—and yet I'll anfwer for it, he has one of the beſt in the univerfe.

Lady. I don't believe your charge.

Sir Luke. Why, though he forgets his ap-pointments with his tradefmen, did you ever hear of his forgetting to go to court when a place was to be difpofed of? Did he ever make a blunder, and fend a bribe to a man out of power? Did he ever forget to kneel before the Prince of this Ifland—or to look in his highnefs's prefence like the fta-tue of Patient-refignation in humble expectation?——

Lady. Dear, Sir Luke——

Sir Luke. Sent from his own country in his very infancy, and brought up in the different

B 2　　　　　　　courts

courts of petty, arbitrary Princes here in Afia; he is the flave of every great man, and the tyrant of every poor one.———

Lady. " Petty Princes !"—'tis well his high-nefs our Sultan does not hear you.

Sir Luke. 'Tis well he does not—don't you repeat what I fay—but you know how all this fine country is harraffed and laid wafte by a fet of Princes, Sultans, as they ftyle themfelves, and I know not what—who are for ever calling out to each other " that's mine," and " that's mine ;"—and " you have no bufinefs here"—and " you have no bufinefs there"—and " *I* have bufinefs every where ;" [*Strutting*] then " give *me* this,"—and " give *me* that ;" and " take this, and take that."
[*makes figns of fighting.*]

Lady. A very elegant defcription truly.

Sir Luke. Why, you know 'tis all matter of fact—and Lord Flint, brought up from his youth amongft thefe people, has not one *trait* of an Eng-lifhman about him—he has imbibed all this coun-try's cruelty, and I dare fay wou'd mind no more feeing me hung up by my thumbs—or made to dance upon a red-hot gridiron.———

Lady. That is one of the tortures I never heard of !—O ! I fhou'd like to fee that of all things !

Sir Luke. Yes—by keeping this man's com-pany, you'll foon be as cruel as he is—he will teach you every vice—a confequential—grave—dull—and yet with that degree of levity, that dares to pay his addreffes to a woman, even before her hufband's face.

Lady. Did not you fay, this minute, his Lord-fhip had not a *trait* of his own country about him ?—

Sir Luke. Well, well—as you 'fay, that laft *is* a *trait* of his own country.

Enter

Enter Servant *and* Lord Flint.

Serv. Lord Flint.— [*Exit* Servant.

Lady. My Lord, I am extremely glad to see you—we were juſt mentioning your name.—

Lord. Were you, indeed, Madam? You do me great honour.

Sir Luke. No, my Lord—no great honour.

Lord. Pardon me, Sir Luke.

Sir Luke. But, I aſſure you, my Lord, what I ſaid, did *myſelf* a great deal of honour.

Lady. Yes, my Lord, and I'll acquaint your Lordſhip what it was. [*going up to him.*

Sir Luke. [*Pulling her aſide*] Why, you wou'd not inform againſt me ſure! Do you know what would be the conſequence? My head muſt anſwer it. [*frightened.*]

Lord. Nay, Sir Luke, I inſiſt upon knowing.

Sir Luke. [*To her*] Huſh—huſh —— no, my Lord, pray excuſe me—your Lordſhip perhaps may think what I ſaid did not come from my heart; and I aſſure you, upon my honour, it did.

Lady. O, yes—that I am ſure it did.

Lord. I am extremely obliged to you. [*bowing.*

Sir Luke. O, no, my Lord, not at all—not at all.—[*aſide to her.*] I'll be extremely obliged to *you*, if you will hold your tongue—Pray, my Lord, are you engaged out to dinner to-day? for her Ladyſhip and I dine out.

Lady. Yes, my Lord, and we ſhould be happy to find your Lordſhip of the party.

Lord. " Engaged out to dinner"?—egad very likely—very likely—but if I am—I have poſitively forgotten where.

Lady. We are going to——

Lord. No—I think (now you put me in mind

of

of it) I think I have company to dine with me—
I am either going out to dinner, or have company
to dine with me ; but I really can't tell which—
however, my people know——but I can't call to
mind.—

Sir Luke. Perhaps your Lordſhip *has* dined ;
can you recollect that ?

Lord. No, no—I have not dined——what's
o'clock ?

Lady. Perhaps, my Lord, you have not breakfaſted.

Lord. O, yes, I've breakfaſted—I think ſo—
but upon my word theſe things are very hard to
remember.

Sir Luke. They are indeed, my Lord—and I
wiſh all my family wou'd entirely forget them.

Lord. What did your Ladyſhip ſay was
o'clock ?

Lady. Exactly twelve, my Lord.

Lord. Bleſs me ! I ought to have been ſome
where elſe then—an abſolute engagement.—I have
broke my word—a poſitive appointment.

Lady. Shall I ſend a ſervant ?

Lord. No, no, no, no—by no means—it can't
be helped now—and they know my unfortunate
failing—beſides, I'll beg their pardon, and I truſt
that will be ample ſatisfaction.

Lady. You are very good, my Lord, not to
leave us.

Lord. I cou'd not think of leaving you ſo ſoon,
Madam—the happineſs I enjoy here is *ſuch*—

Sir Luke. And very likely were your Lordſhip
to go away now, you might never recollect to
come again.

Enter

Enter Servant.

Serv. A Gentleman, Sir, juſt come from on board an Engliſh veſſel, ſays, he has letters to preſent to you.

Sir Luke. Shew him in—[*Exit* Servant.] He has brought his character too, I ſuppoſe—and left it *behind,* too, I ſuppoſe.

Enter Mr. Twineall, *in a faſhionable undreſs.*

Twi. Sir Luke, I have the honour of preſenting to you, [*Gives letters*] one from my Lord Cleland—one from Sir Thomas Shoeſtring—one from Colonel Fril.

Sir Luke. [*Aſide*] Who in the name of wonder have my friends recommended?—[*reads while Lord* Flint *and the Lady talk apart*] No—as I live, he is a gentleman, and the ſon of a Lord—[*going to Lady* Tremor.] My dear, that is a gentleman, notwithſtanding his appearance—don't laugh—but let me introduce you to him.

Lady. A gentleman! certainly—I did not look at him before—but now I can perceive it.

Sir Luke. Mr. Twineall, give me leave to introduce Lady Tremor to you, and my Lord Flint—this, my Lord, is the Honourable Mr. Twineall from England, who will do me the favour to remain in my houſe, till he is ſettled to his mind in ſome poſt here. [*They bow.*] I beg your pardon, Sir, for the ſomewhat cool reception Lady Tremor and I gave you at firſt—but I dare ſay her Ladyſhip was under the ſame miſtake as myſelf—and I muſt own I took you at firſt ſight for ſomething very different from the perſon you prove to be—for really no Engliſh ſhips have arrived in this harbour for

                              theſe

thefe five years paft, and the drefs of us Englifh
gentlemen is fo much altered fince that time—

Twi. But, I hope, Sir Luke, if it is, the alteration meets with your approbation.

Lady. O ! to be fure—it is extremely elegant
. and becoming.

Sir Luke. Yes, my dear, I don't doubt but you
think fo ; for I remember you ufed to make your
favourite monkey wear juft fuch a jacket, when
he went out a vifiting.

Twin. Was he your favourite, Madam ?—Sir,
you are very obliging. [*Bowing to Sir Luke.*]

Sir Luke. My Lord, if it were poffible for your
Lordfhip to call to your *remembrance* fuch a trifle—

Lady. Dear Sir Luke——   [*Pulling him.*

Lord. Egad, I believe I do call to my remembrance—[*Gravely confidering.*]—Not, I affure you,
Sir, that I perceive any great refemblance—or, if
it was fo—I dare fay it is merely in the drefs——
which I muft own ftrikes me as moft ridiculous—
very ridiculous indeed.——

Twi. My Lord !

Lord. I beg pardon, if I have faid any thing
that——Lady Tremor, what did I fay ?——
make my apology, if I have faid any thing im-
.proper—you know my unhappy failing.

[*Goes up the ftage.*

Lady. [*to Twineall.*] Sir, his Lordfhip has made
a miftake in the word " ridiculous," which I am
fure he did not mean to fay—but he is apt to make
ufe of one word for another—his Lordfhip has
been fo long out of England, that he may be faid in
fome meafure to have forgotten his native language.

[*His Lordfhip all this time appears confequen-
tially abfent.*

Twi. And you have perfectly explained, Madam—indeed I ought to have been convinced,
without

without your explanation, that if his Lordſhip made uſe of the word *ridiculous* (even intentionally) that the word had now changed its former ſenſe, and was become a mode to expreſs ſatiſfaction—or his Lordſhip wou'd not have made uſe of it in the very forcible manner he did, to a perfect ſtranger.

Sir Luke. What, Mr. Twineall, have you new modes, new faſhions for *words* too in England, as well as for dreſſes ?—and are you equally extravagant in their adoption ?

Lady. I never heard, Sir Luke, but that the faſhion of words varied, as well as the faſhion of every thing elſe.

Twi. But what is moſt extraordinary—we have now a faſhion in England, of ſpeaking without any words at all.

Lady. Pray, Sir, how is that ?

Sir Luke. Ay, do, Mr. Twineall, teach my wife, and I ſhall be very much obliged to you—it will be a great accompliſhment. Even you, my Lord, ought to be attentive to this faſhion.

Twi. Why, Madam, for inſtance, when a gentleman is aſked a queſtion which is either troubleſome or improper to anſwer, you don't ſay you *won't* anſwer it, even though you ſpeak to an inferior——but you ſay——" really it appears to me e-e-e-e-e—[*mutters and ſhrugs*]—that is—mo-mo-mo-mo-mo—[*mutters*]—if you ſee the thing—for my part——te-te-te-te——and that's all I can tell about it at *preſent.*

Sir Luke. And you have told nothing !

Twi. Nothing upon earth.

Lady. But mayn't one gueſs what you mean?

Twi. O, yes—perfectly at liberty to gueſs.

Sir Luke. Well, I'll be ſhot if I *could* gueſs.

Twi. And again—when an impertinent pedant

C   aſks

afks you a queftion that you know nothing about, and it may not be convenient to fay fo—you anfwer *boldly*, " why really, Sir, my opinion *is*, that the Greek poet—he-he-he-he—[*mutters*]—we-we-we-we—you fee—if his idea was—and if the Latin tranflator—mis-mis mis-mis——[*fhrugs*]——that I fhou'd think—in my humble opinion—but the Doctor *may* know better than I."——

Sir Luke. The Doctor muft know very little elfe.

Twi. Or in cafe of a duel, where one does not care to fay who was right, or who was wrong—you anfwer—" *This*, Sir, is the ftate of the matter—Mr. F— came firft—te-te-te-te—on that—be-be-be-be—if the other—in fhort—[*whifpers*]—whis-whis-whis-whis"——

Sir Luke. What?

Twi. " There, now you have it—there 'tis—but don't fay a word about it—or, if you do—don't fay it come from me."—

Lady. Why, you have not told a word of the ftory!

Twi. But that your auditor muft not fay to you —that's not the fafhion—he never tells you that——he may fay—" You have not made yourfelf *perfectly* clear;"—or he may fay—" He muft have the matter *more particularly* pointed out fomewhere elfe;"—but that is all the auditor can fay with good breeding.

Lady. A very pretty method indeed to fatisfy one's curiofity!

Enter Servant.

Serv. Mr. Hafwell.

Sir Luke. This is a countryman of ours, Mr. Twincall, and a very good man I affure you.

Enter

Enter Mr. Hafwell.

Sir Luke. Mr. Hafwell, how do you do?
            [Warmly.

Haf. Sir Luke, I am glad to fee you.——Lady
Tremor, how do you do? *[He bows to the reft.*

Lady. O, Mr. Hafwell, I am extremely glad
you are come—here is a young adventurer juft arrived from England, who has been giving us fuch
a ftrange account of all that's going on there.
         [Introducing Twineall.

Haf. Sir, you are welcome to India.
       [Sir Luke whifpers Hafwell.

Indeed!—*his* fon.

Lady. Do, Mr. Hafwell, talk to him—he can
give you great information.

Haf. I am glad of it—I fhall then hear many
things I am impatient to become acquainted with.
[Goes up to Twineall.] Mr. Twineall, I have the
honour of knowing his Lordfhip, your father, extremely well—he holds his feat in Parliament ftill,
I prefume?

Twi. He does, Sir.

Haf. And your uncle, Sir Charles?

Twi. Both, Sir—both in Parliament ftill.

Haf. Pray, Sir, has any act in behalf of the
poor clergy taken place yet?

Twi. In behalf of the poor clergy, Sir?—I'll
tell you—I'll tell you, Sir.——As to that act—
concerning—*[fhrugs and mutters]*—em-em-em-em
—the Committee—em em—ways and means—
hee-hee—I affure you, Sir—te-te-te—
   [Sir Luke, Lady, and Lord Flint laugh.
My father and my uncle both think fo, I affure
you.

Haf. Think *how*, Sir?

Sir Luke. Nay, that's not good breeding—you muſt aſk no more queſtions.

Haſ. Why not?

Sir Luke. Becauſe—we-we we-we—[*mimicks*]—he knows nothing about it.

Haſ. What, Sir—not know?

Twi. Yes, Sir, perfectly acquainted with every thing that paſſes in the houſe—but I aſſure you, that when they come to be reported——but, Sir Luke, now permit me, in my turn, to make a few inquiries concerning the ſtate of this country.

[*Sir Luke ſtarts, and fixes his eyes ſuſpiciouſly on Lord Flint.*

Sir Luke. Why, one does not like to ſpeak much about the country one lives in—but, Mr. Haſwell, you have been viſiting our encampments; *you* may tell us what is going on there.

Lady. Pray, Mr. Haſwell, is it true that the Sultan cut off the head of one of his wives the other day becauſe ſhe ſaid " I won't?"

Sir Luke. Do, my dear, be ſilent.

Lady. I won't.

Sir Luke. O, that the Sultan had you inſtead of me!

Lady. And with my head off, I ſuppoſe?

Sir Luke. No, my dear; in that ſtate, I ſhou'd have no objection to you myſelf.

Lady. [*Aſide to Sir Luke.*] Now, I'll frighten you ten times more.—But, Mr. Haſwell, I am told there are many perſons ſuſpected of diſaffection to the preſent Sultan, who have been lately, by his orders, arreſted, and ſold to ſlavery, notwithſtanding there was no proof againſt them produced.

Haſ. Proof!——in a State ſuch as this, the charge is quite ſufficient.

Sir Luke. [*In apparent agonies, wiſhing to turn the*

the difcourfe.] Well, my Lord, and how does your Lordfhip find yourfelf this afternoon ?—this morning, 1 mean—Blefs my foul ! why I begin to be as forgetful as your Lordfhip.

[*Smiling and fawning.*

Lady. How I pity the poor creatures !

Sir Luke. [*Afide to Lady.*] Take care what you fay before that tool of ftate—look at him, and tremble for your head.

Lady. Look at him, and tremble for *yours*—and fo, Mr. Hafwell, all this is true ?—and fome people, of confequence too, I am told, dragged from their homes, and fent to flavery merely on fufpicion ?

Haf. Yet, lefs do I pity thofe, than fome, whom prifons and dungeons crammed before, are yet prepared to receive.

Lord. Mr. Hafwell, fuch is the Sultan's pleafure.

Sir Luke. Will your Lordfhip take a turn in the garden ? it looks from this door very pleafant ; —does not it ?

Lady. But pray, Mr. Hafwell, has not the Sultan fent for you to attend at his palace this morning ?

Haf. He has, Madam.

Lady. There ! I heard he had, but Sir Luke faid not.—I am told he thinks himfelf under the greateft obligations to you.

Haf. The report has flattered me—but if his highnefs *fhou'd* think himfelf under obligations, I can readily point a way, by which he may acquit himfelf of them.

Lady. In the mean time, I am fure, you feel for thofe poor fufferers.

Haf. [*With ftifled emotion.*] Sir Luke, good morning to you — I call'd upon fome trifling bufinefs, but I have out-ftaid my time, and therefore

fore I'll call again in a couple of hours—Lady
Tremor, good morning—my Lord—Mr. Twineall—[*Bows, and exit.*

Twi. Sir Luke, your garden *does* look so di-
vinely beautiful—

Sir Luke. Come, my Lord, will you take a
turn in it? Come Mr. Twineall—come my dear—
[*taking her hand.*] I can't think what business Mr.
Haswell has to speak to me upon—for my part, I
am quite a plain man—and busy myself about no
one's affairs, except my own—but I dare say your
Lordship has forgot all we have been talking
about.

Lord. If you permit me, Sir Luke, I'll hand
the Lady.

Sir Luke. Certainly, my Lord, if you please—
come, Mr. Twineall, and I'll conduct you.

[*Exeunt.*

END OF THE FIRST ACT.

ACT

ACT II.

SCENE I. *An Apartment at Sir Luke Tremor's.*

Enter Twineall *and* Meanright.

Twi. MY dear friend, after so long a separation, how glad I am to meet you!—but how devilish unlucky that you shou'd, on the very day of my arrival, be going to set sail for another part of the world! yet before you go, I must beg a favour of you—you know Sir Luke and his family perfectly well, I dare say?

Mean. I think so—I have been in his house near six years.

Twi. The very person on earth I wanted!—Sir Luke has power here, I suppose?—a word from him might do a man some service perhaps?
[*significantly.*

Mean. Why, yes; I don't know a man that has more influence at a certain place.

Twin. And her Ladyship seems a very clever gentlewoman?

Mean. Very.

Twi. And I have a notion they think *me* very clever.

Mean. I dare say they do.

Twi. Yes—but I mean *very* clever.

Mean. No doubt!

Twi. But, my dear friend, you must help me to make them think better of me still—and when

my

my fortune is made, I'll make *yours*—for when I once become acquainted with people's difpofitions, their little weaknefles, foibles and faults, I can wind, twift, twine, and get into the corner of every one's heart, and lie fo fnug, they can't know I'm there, till they want to pull me out, and find 'tis impoffible.

Mean.   Excellent talent!

Twi.   Is not it? and now, my dear friend, do you inform me of the fecret difpofitions, and propenfities of every one in this family, and of all their connections.—What Lady values herfelf upon one qualification, and what Lady upon another?—What Gentleman will like to be told of his accomplifhments? or what man would rather hear of his wife's, or his daughter's?—or of his horfes? or of his dogs?—now, my dear Ned, acquaint me with all this—and within a fortnight I will become the moft neceffary rafcal——not a creature fhall know how to exift without me.

Mean.   Why fuch a man as you ought to have made your fortune in England.

Twi.   No—my father, and my three uncles monopolized all the great men themfelves; and wou'd never introduce me where I was likely to become their rival—This—this is the very fpot for me to difplay my genius—But then I muft penetrate the people firft—and you will kindly fave me that trouble.—Come, give me all their characters—all their little propenfities—all their whims—in fhort, all I am to praife—and all I am to avoid praifing,—in order to endear myfelf to them. [*Takes out tablets.*] Come—begin with Sir Luke.

Mean.   Sir Luke—values himfelf more upon perfonal bravery, than upon any thing elfe.

Twi.

Twi. Thank you, my dear friend—thank you. [*Writes*] Was he ever in the army?

Mean. Oh yes—befieged a capital fortrefs, a few years ago—and now, the very name of a battle or a great general tickles his vanity, and he takes all the praifes you can lavifh upon the fubject as compliments to himfelf.

Twi. Thank you—thank you a thoufand times —[*Writes.*] I'll mention a battle very foon.

Mean. Not directly.

Twi. O, no—let me alone for time and place —go on, my friend—go on—her Ladyfhip—

Mean. Defcended from the ancient kings of Scotland.

Twi. You don't fay fo!

Mean. And though fhe is fo nicely fcrupulous as never to mention the word genealogy, yet I have feen her agitation fo great, when the advantages of high birth have been extoll'd, fhe could fcarcely withhold her fentiments of triumph; which in order to difguife, fhe has affumed a difdain for all " vain titles—empty founds—and idle pomp."

Twi. Thank you—thank you—this is a moft excellent *trait* of the Lady's—[*Writes.*] " Pedigree of the kings of Scotland?" O, I have her at once.

Mean. Yet do it nicely—oblique touches, rather than open explanations.

Twi. Let me alone for that.

Mean. She has, I know, in her poffeffion— but I dare fay fhe wou'd not fhow it you, nay, on the contrary, would even *affect* to be highly offended, if you were to mention it—and yet it certainly would flatter her, to know you were acquainted with her having it.

Twi. What—what—what is it?

Mean. A large old-fafhioned wig—which Mal-

D   colm

colin the third or fourth, her great anceftor, wore
when he was crowned at Scone, in the year ——

Twi. I'll mention it.

Mean. Take care.

Twi. O, let me alone for the *manner*.

Mean. She'll pretend to be angry.

Twi. That I am prepared for.—Pray who is
my Lord Flint?

Mean. A deep man—and a great favourite at
court.

Twi. Indeed!—how am I to pleafe him?

Mean. By infinuations againft the *prefent* Sultan.

Twi. How!

Mean. With all his pretended attachment, his
heart——

Twi. Are you *fure* of it?

Mean. Sure :—he blinds Sir Luke, (who by
the bye is no great politician) but I know his Lordfhip—and if he thought he was fure of his ground
—(and he thinks he *fhall* be fure, of it foon)—
then—

Twi. I'll infinuate myfelf and join his party—
but, in the mean time, preferve good terms with
Sir Luke, in cafe any thing fhou'd fall in my way
there.—Who is Mr. Hafwell?

Mean. He pretends to be a man of principle
and fentiment—flatter him on that.

Twi. The eafieft thing in the world—no people like flattery better than fuch as he.—They
will bear even to hear their *vices* praifed.—I will
myfelf undertake to praife the vices of a man of
fentiment till he fhall think them fo many virtues.
—You have mentioned no Ladies, but the Lady
of the houfe yet.

Mean. There is no other Lady, except a pretty
girl who came over from England, about two years
ago, for a hufband, and not fucceeding in another

part

part of the country, is now recommended to this house—and has been here three or four months.

Twi. Let me alone, to pleafe her.

Mean. Yes—I believe you are fkilled.

Twi. For the art of flattery, no one more.

Mean. But damn it—it is not a liberal art.

Twi. It is a great fcience, notwithftanding—and ftudied, at prefent, by all the connoiffeurs.—Zounds! I have ftaid a long time—I can't attend to any more characters at prefent—Sir Luke and his Lady will think me inattentive, if I don't join them—Shall I fee you again?—if not—I wifh you a pleafant voyage—I'll make the moft of what you have told me—you'll hear I'm a great man—God blefs you!—good bye!—you'll hear I'm a great man.   [*Exit.*

Mean. And, if I am not miftaken, I fhall hear you are turned out of the houfe before to-morrow morning. O, Twineall! exactly the *reverfe* of every character have you now before you—the greateft misfortune in the life of Sir Luke has been, flying from his army in the midft of an engagement, and a moft humiliating degradation in confequence, which makes him fo feelingly alive on the fubject of a battle, that nothing but his want of courage can fecure my friend Twineall's life for venturing to name the fubject—then Lord Flint, firmly *attached* to the *intereft* of the Sultan, will be all on fire, when he hears of open difaffection—but moft of all her Ladyfhip! whofe father was a grocer, and uncle, a noted advertifing " Periwig-maker on a new conftruction." She will run mad to hear of births, titles, and long pedigrees.—Poor Twineall! little doft thou think what is prepared for thee.—There is Mr. Hafwell too—but to him have I fent you to be reclaimed—to him,—who, free from faults, or even foibles,

of

of his own, has yet more potently the blessing
given, of tenderness for ours.   [*Exit.*

SCENE II. *The inside of a Prison.*

Several Prisoners dispersed in different situations.

Enter Keeper *and* Haswell *with lights.*

Keep. This way, Sir—the prisons this way are
more extensive still—you seem to feel for these un-
thinking men—but they are a set of unruly people, whom no severity can make such as they ought
to be.

Haf. And wou'd not gentleness, or mercy, do
you think, reclaim them?

Keep. That I can't say—we never try those
means in this part of the world—that man yonder,
suspected of disaffection, is sentenced to be here
for life, unless his friends can lay down a large
sum by way of penalty, which he finds they cannot
do, and he is turned melancholy.

Haf. [*After a pause.*] Who is that? [*To another.*

Keep. He has been try'd for heading an insur-
rection, and acquitted.

Haf. What keeps him here?

Keep. Fees due to the Court—a debt contracted
while he proved his innocence.

Haf. Lead on, my friend—let us go to some
other part.   [*Putting his hand to his eyes.*

Keep. In this ward, we are going to, are the
prisoners, who by some small reserve—some little
secreted stock when they arrived—or by the bounty
of some friend who visit them —— or such-
like fortunate circumstance, are in a less dismal
place.

Haf. Lead on.

                                        Keep.

Keep. But ftop—put on this cloak, for, before we arrive at the place I mention, we muft pafs a damp vault, which to thofe who are not ufed to it—[Hafwell *puts on the cloak*]—or will you poftpone your vifit?

Haf. No—go on.

Keep. Alas! who wou'd fuppofe you had been ufed to fee fuch places!—you look concerned—vext to fee the people fuffer—I wonder you fhou'd come, when you feem to think fo much about them.

Haf. Oh! that, that is the very reafon.

[*Exit, following the Keeper.*

[Zedan, *a tawny Indian Prifoner, follows them, ftealing out, as if intent on fomething.*]

Two Prifoners walk flowly down the Stage.

1ft Prif. Who is this man?

2d Prif. From Britain—I have feen him once before.

1ft Prif. He looks pale—he has no heart.

2d Prif. I believe, a pretty large one.

Re-enter Zedan.

Zed. Brother, a word with you. [*To the 1ft Prifoner, the other retires*] as the ftranger and our keeper paffed by the paffage, a noxious vapour put out the light, and as they groped along I purloined *this* from the ftranger—[*Shews a pocket-book*] fee it contains two notes will pay our ranfom.

[*Shewing the notes.*

1ft Prif. A treafure—our certain ranfom!

Zed. Liberty! our wives, our children, and our friends, will thefe papers purchafe.

1ft Prif. What a bribe! our keeper may rejoice too,

Zed.

Zed. And then the pleasure it will be to hear the stranger fret, and complain for his loss!—O, how my heart loves to see sorrow!—Misery such as I have known, on men who spurn me—who treat me as if (in my own Island) I had no friends that loved me—no servants that paid me honour —no children that revered me—who forget I am a husband—a father—nay, a *man.*— ✳

1st Prif. Conceal your thoughts—conceal your treasure too—or the Briton's complaint—

Zed. Will be in vain—our keeper will conclude the bribe must come to him, at last—and therefore make no great search for it—here, in the corner of my belt [*Puts up the pocket-book*] 'twill be secure— Come this way, and let us indulge our pleasant prospect.   [*They retire, and the scene closes.*

SCENE III.   *Another part of the Prison.*

A kind of sopha with an old man sleeping upon it— Elvirus *fitting attentively by him.*

Enter Keeper *and* Hafwell.

Keep. That young man, you see there, watching his aged father as he sleeps, by the help of fees gains his admission—and he never quits the place, except to go and purchase cordials for the old man, who, (though healthy and strong when he first became a prisoner) is now become ill and languid.

Haf. Are they from Europe?

Keep. No—but descended from Europeans— see how the youth holds his father's hand!—I have sometimes caught him bathing it with tears.

Haf. I'll speak to the young man. [*Going to him.*

Keep. *He* will speak as soon as he sees me—he has sent a petition to the Sultan about his father,
                                                      and

and never fails to inquire if a reply is come. [*They approach*—Elvirus *starts, and comes forward*]

Elv. [*To* Hafwell] Sir, do you come from the Court? has the Sultan received my humble fupplication? Can you tell?—foftly—let not my father hear you fpeak.

Haf. I come but as a ftranger, to fee the prifon.

Elv. No anfwer yet, keeper?

Keep. No—I told you it was in vain to write—they never read petitions fent from prifons—their hearts are hardened to fuch worn-out tales of forrow. [Elvirus *turns towards his Father and weeps.*

Haf. Pardon me, Sir—but what is the requeft you are thus denied?

Elv. Behold my father! but three months has he been confined here; and yet—unlefs he breathes a purer air—O, if *you* have influence at Court, Sir, pray reprefent what paffes in this dreary prifon—what paffes in my heart.——My fupplication is to remain a prifoner here, while my father, releafed, fhall be permitted to retire to humble life; and never more take arms in a caufe the Sultan may fufpect—which engagement broken, *my life* fhall be the forfeit.—Or if the Sultan wou'd allow me to ferve him as a foldier—

Haf. You would fight againft the party your father fought for?

Elv. [*Starting.*] No—but in the forefts—or on the defert fands—amongft thofe flaves who are fent to battle with the wild Indians—there I wou'd go—and earn the boon I afk——or in the mines—

Haf. Give me your name—I will, at leaft, prefent your fuit—and, perhaps—

Elv. Sir! do you think it is likely? Joyful hearing!

Haf. Nay, be not too hafty in your hopes—I
cannot

cannot *anſwer* for my ſucceſs. [*Repeats*] " Your
" father humbly implores to be releaſed from
" priſon—and, in his ſtead, *you* take his chains—
" or, for the Sultan's ſervice, fight as a ſlave,
" or dig in his mines ?"

Elv. Exactly, Sir—that is the petition—I thank
you, Sir.

Keep. You don't know, young man, what it *is*
to dig in mines—or fight againſt foes, who make
their priſoners die by unheard-of tortures.

Elv. *You* do not know, Sir, what it *is,*—to ſee
a parent ſuffer.

Haſ. [*Writing*] Your name, Sir ?

Elv. Elvirus Caſimir.—

Haſ. Your father's ?

Elv. The ſame—one who followed agriculture
in the fields of Symria—but, induced by the call
of freedom—

Haſ. How ? have a care.

Elv. No—his ſon, by the call of nature, ſup-
plicates his freedom.

Keep. The rebel, you find, breaks out.

Elv. [*Aſide to the Keeper.*] Silence—ſilence !
he forgives it—don't remind him of it—don't
undo my hopes.

Haſ. I will ſerve you if I can.

Elv. And I will merit it—indeed I will—you
ſhall not complain of me—I will be—

Haſ. Retire—I truſt you. [Elvirus *bows lowly,
and retires.*]

Keep. Yonder cell contains a female priſoner.

Haſ. A female priſoner !

Keep. Without a friend or comforter, ſhe has
exiſted there theſe many years—nearly fifteen.

Haſ. Is it poſſible !

Keep. Wou'd you wiſh to ſee her ?

Haſ. If it won't give her pain.

Keep.

Keep. At leaſt, ſhe'll not reſent it—for ſhe ſeldom complains, except in moans to herſelf—[*Goes to the cell.*] Lady, here is one come to viſit all the priſoners—pleaſe to appear before him.

Haſ. I thank you—you ſpeak with reverence and reſpect to her.

Keep. She has been of ſome note, though now ſo totally unfriended—at leaſt, we *think* ſhe has, from her gentle manners; and our governor is in the daily expectation of ſome liberal ranſom for her, which makes her impriſonment without a hope of releaſe, till that day arrives—[*Going to the cell*]—Lend me your hand—you are weak. [*He leads her from the cell—ſhe appears faint—and as if the light affected her eyes—*Haſwell *pulls off his hat, and, after a pauſe—*

Haſ. I fear you are not in health, Lady? ——
[*She looks at him ſolemnly for ſome time.*

Keep. Speak—Madam, ſpeak.

Priſ. No—not very well. [*Faintingly.*

Haſ. Where are your friends? When do you expect your ranſom?

Priſ. [*Shaking her head.*] Never.

Keep. She perſiſts to ſay ſo; thinking by that declaration, we ſhall releaſe her *without* a ranſom.

Haſ. Is that your motive?

Priſ. I know no motive for a falſehood.

Haſ. I was to blame—pardon me.

Keep. Your anſwers are ſomewhat prouder than uſual. [*He retires up the ſtage.*

Priſ. They are.—[*To* Haſwell] Forgive me—I am mild with all of theſe—but from a countenance like yours—I could not bear reproach.

Haſ. You flatter me.

Priſ. Alas! Sir, and what have I to hope from ſuch a meaneſs?—You do not come to ranſom me.

E   *Haſ.*

Haf. Perhaps I do.

Prif. Oh! do not fay fo—unlefs—unlefs—I am not to be deceived—pardon in your turn this fufpicion—but when I have fo much to hope for—when the fun, the air, fields, woods, and all that wonderous world, wherein I have been fo happy, is in profpect; forgive me, if the vaft hope makes me fear.

Haf. Unlefs your ranfom is fixed at fomething beyond my power to give, I *will* releafe you.

Prif. Releafe me! Benevolent!

Haf. How fhall I mark you down in my petition? [*Takes out his book.*] what name?

Prif. 'Tis almoft blotted from my memory.
[*Weeping.*

Keep. It is of little note—a female prifoner, taken with the rebel party, and in thefe cells confined for fifteen years.

Prif. During which time I have demeaned myfelf with all humility to my governors—neither have I diftracted my fellow prifoners with a complaint that might recall to their memory their own unhappy fate—I have been obedient, patient; and cherifhed hope to chear me with vain dreams, while defpair poffefs'd my reafon.

Haf. Retire—I will prefent the picture you have given.

Prif. Succeed too—or, never let me fee you more— [*She goes up the ftage.*

Haf. You never fhall.

Prif. [*Returns*] Or, if you fhou'd mifcarry in your views [for who forms plans that do not fometimes fail?] I will not reproach you even to *myfelf*——no—nor will I fuffer *much* from the difappointment—merely that you may not have, what I fuffer, to account for. [*Exit to her cell.*

Haf. Excellent mind!
Keep.

Keep. . In this cell—   [*Going to another.*
Haf. No— take me away—I have enough to
do—I dare not fee more at prefent.—   [*Exeunt.*

SCENE IV. *The former Prifon Scene.*

Enter Zedan,

Zed. They are coming—I'll ftand here in his
fight, that, fhou'd he mifs what I have taken,
he'll not fufpect me, but fuppofe it is one who has
hid himfelf.

Enter Keeper *and* Hafwell.

Keep. [*To* Zedan] What makes you here ?—ftill
moping by yourfelf, and lamenting for your family ?—[*To* Hafwell] that man, the moft feroci-
ous I ever met with—laments, fometimes even
with tears, the feparation from his wife and children.

Haf. [*Going to him*] I am forry for you, friend ;
[Zedan *looks fullen and morofe.*] I pity you.

Keep. Yes—he had a pleafant hamlet on the
neighbouring ifland -- plenty of fruits — clear
fprings—and wholefome roots—and now complains bitterly of his repafts—four rice, and
muddy water.   [*Exit Keeper.*

Haf. Poor man ! bear your forrows nobly—
and as we are alone—no miferable eye to grudge
the favour—[*Looking round*] take this trifle—
[*Gives money*] it will at leaft make your meals better for a few fhort weeks—till Heaven may pleafe
to favour you with a lefs fharp remembrance of
the happinefs you have loft—Farewell. [*Going.*]
[Zedan *catches hold of him, and taking the pocket-book
from his belt, puts it into* Hafwell's *hand.*]

E 2   *Haf.*

Haf. What's this?

Zed. I meant to gain my liberty with it—but I will not vex you.

Haf. How came you by it?

Zed. Stole it—and wou'd have ftabb'd you too, had you been alone—but I am glad I did not—Oh! I am glad I did not.

Haf. You like me then?

Zed. [*Shakes his head and holds his heart.*] 'Tis fomething that I never felt before—it makes me like not only you, but all the world befides—the love of my family was confined to them alone; but this makes me feel I could love even my enemies.

Haf. Oh, nature! grateful! mild! gentle! and forgiving!—worft of tyrants they who, by hard ufage, drive you to be cruel!

Enter Keeper.

Keep. The lights are ready, Sir, through the dark paffage—[*To* Zedan.] Go to your fellows.

Haf. [*To* Zedan.] Farewell—we will meet again.

[Zedan *exit on one fide*, Hafwell *and* Keeper *exeunt on the other.*

END OF THE SECOND ACT.

ACT

A C T III.

SCENE I. *An Apartment at* Sir Luke Tremor's.

Enter Sir Luke *and* Aurelia.

Sir Luke.

WHY, then Aurelia, (though I never mention'd it to my Lady Tremor) my friend wrote me word, he had reason to suppose your affections were improperly fixed upon a young gentleman in that neighbourhood; and this was his reason for wishing you to leave that place to come hither —and this continual dejection convinces me my friend was not mistaken—answer me—can you say he was?

Aur. Why, then, Sir Luke, candidly to confess—

Sir Luke. Nay, no tears—why in tears? for a husband? be comforted—we'll get you one ere long, I warrant.

Aur. Dear, Sir Luke, how can you imagine I am in tears because I have not a husband, while you see Lady Tremor every day in tears for the very opposite cause?

Sir Luke. No matter—women like a husband through pride—and I have known a woman marry from that very motive, even a man she has been ashamed of.

Aur. Why, then I dare say, poor Lady Tremor married from pride.

3

Sir

Sir Luke. Yes;—and I'll let her know pride is painful..

Aur. But, Sir, her Ladyſhip's philoſophy—

Sir Luke. She has no philoſophy.

Enter Lady Tremor *and* Twineall.

Sir Luke. Where is his Lordſhip ? What have you done with him ?

Lady. He's ſpeaking a word to Mr. Meanright about his paſſport to England.—Did you mean me, Sir Luke, that had no philoſophy ? I proteſt, I have a great deal.

Sir Luke. When ? where did you ſhew it ?

Lady. Why, when the ſervant at my Lady Griſſel's threw a whole urn of boiling water upon your legs, did I give any proofs of female weakneſs ? did I faint, ſcream, or even ſhed a tear ?

Sir Luke. No—no—very true—and while I lay ſprawling on the carpet, I could ſee you fanning and holding the ſmelling bottle to the Lady of the houſe, begging her not to make herſelf uneaſy, " for that the accident was of no manner of con- " ſequence."

Aur. Dear Sir, don't be angry ;—I am ſure her Ladyſhip ſpoke as ſhe thought.

Sir Luke. I ſuppoſe ſhe did, Miſs.

Aur. I mean—ſhe thought the accident might be eaſily got the better of—She thought you might be eaſily recovered.

Lady. No, indeed, I did not—but I thought Sir Luke had frequently charged me with the want of patience; and that moment, the very thing in the world I cou'd have wiſhed, happened —on purpoſe to give me an opportunity to prove his accuſation falſe.

Sir Luke. Very well, Madam—but did not the whole

whole company cry shame on your behaviour? did not they say, it was not the conduct of a wife?

Lady. Only our particular acquaintance cou'd say so—for the rest of the company, I am sure, did not take me to be your wife—thank Heaven, our appearances never betray that secret—do you think we look like the same flesh and blood?

Sir Luke. That day, in particular, we did not —for I remember you had been no less than three hours at your toilet.

Aur. And, indeed, Sir Luke, if you were to use milk of roses, and several other little things of that kind, you can't think how much more like a fine gentleman you wou'd look.—Such things as those make, almost, all the difference there is between you and such a gentleman as Mr. Twineall.

Twi. No, pardon me, Madam—a face like *mine* may use those things—but in Sir Luke's, they wou'd entirely destroy that fine martial appearance —[*Sir Luke looks confounded.*] which women as well as men admire—for, as valour is the first ornament of *our* sex——

Lady. What are you saying, Mr. Twineall? [*Aside.*] I'll keep him on this subject if I can.

Twi. I was going to observe, Madam—that the reputation of a General—which puts me in mind, Sir Luke, of an account I read of a battle—[*He crosses over to Sir Luke, who turns up the Stage in the utmost confusion, and steals out of the room.*]

Lady. Well, Sir—go on—go on—you were going to introduce—

Twi. A battle, Madam—but, Sir Luke is gone!

Lady. Never mind that, Sir—he generally runs away on these occasions.

Sir Luke. [*Coming back.*] What were you saying, Aurelia, about a husband?

Lady.

Lady. She did not fpeak.

Sir Luke. To be fure, Ladies in India do get hufbands very quick.

Twi. Not always—I am told, Sir Luke—— Women of family, [*fixing his eyes ftedfaftly on Lady* Tremor.] indeed, may foon enter into the matrimonial ftate—but the rich men in India, we are told in England, are grown lately very particular with whom they marry, and there is not a man of any repute that will now look upon a woman as a wife, unlefs fhe is defcended from a good family. [*Looking at Lady* Tremor, *who walks up the Stage and fteals off, juft as Sir* Luke *had done before.*

Sir Luke. I am very forry—very forry to fay, Mr. Twineall, that has not been always the cafe.

Twi. Then I am very forry too, Sir Luke; for it is as much impoffible that a woman, who is not born of a good family, can be—

       [*Lady* Tremor *returns.*

Sir Luke. That is juft what I fay—they *cannot* be—

Lady. Sir Luke, let me tell you—

Sir Luke. It does not fignify *telling*, my dear,— you have *proved* it.

Lady. [*To* Twineall.] Sir, let me tell *you*—

Twi. O! O! my dear Madam, 'tis all in vain—there is no fuch thing—it can't be—there is no pleading againft conviction—a perfon of low birth muft, in every particular, be a terrible creature.

Sir Luke. [*Going to her.*] A terrible creature! a terrible creature!

Lady. Here comes my Lord Flint—I'll appeal to him.

           Enter

Enter Lord Flint.

Sir Luke. [*Going to him.*] My Lord, I was say-ing, as proof that our great Sultan, who now fills this throne, is no impoftor, (as the rebel party wou'd infinuate) no low-born man, but of the Royal Stock; his conduct palpably evinces—for, had he not been nobly born, we fhou'd have be-held the Plebeian burfting forth upon all occafions [*Looking at Lady* Tremor] and then, Heaven help all thofe who had had any dealings with him !

Lady. Provoking !   [*Goes up the ftage.*

Lord. Sir Luke, is there a doubt of the Em-peror's birth and title ? he is the real Sultan, de-pend upon it—it furprifes me to hear you talk with the fmalleft uncertainty.

Twi. O, Sir Luke, I wonder at it too, [*Afide to Lord* Flint.] and yet, damn me, my Lord, if I have not my doubts.   [*Lord* Flint *ftarts.*

Sir Luke. I, my Lord ? far be it from me ! I was only faying what other people faid ; for my part *I* never harboured a doubt of the kind.— [*Afide.*] My head begins to nod, only for that word—pray Heaven, I may die with it on !—I fhou'd not like to lofe my head—nor fhou'd I like to die by a bullet—nor by a fmall fword—and a cannon ball wou'd be as difagreeable, as any thing, I know—it is very odd—but I never yet could make up my mind, in what manner I fhou'd like to go out of the world.   [*During this fpeech.* Twineall *is paying court to Lord* Flint ; *they come for-ward and Sir* Luke *retires.*

Lord. Your temerity aftonifhes me !

Twi. I muft own, my Lord, I feel fomewhat aukward in faying it to your Lordfhip—but my own heart—my own confcience—my own fenti-ments—they *are* my own—and they are dear to

F   me.

me.—And so it is—the Sultan does not appear to
be [*With significance.*] that great man some people think him.

Lord. Sir, you astonish me—pray what is your
name? I have forgotten it.

Twi. Twineall, my Lord—the honourable Henry
Twineall—your Lordship does me great honour
to ask — arrived this morning from England,
as your Lordship may remember—in the ship
Mercury, my Lord—and all the officers on board
speaking with the highest admiration and warm-
est terms of your Lordship's official character.

Lord. Why, then, Mr. Twineall, I am very
sorry—

Twi. And so am I, my Lord, that your sentiments and mine shou'd so far disagree, as I *know*
they do.—I am not unacquainted with your firm
adherence to the Emperor—but I am unused to
disguise my thoughts—I cou'd not, if I wou'd—
I have no little views—no sinister motives—no
plots—no intrigues—no schemes of preferment,—
and I verily believe that if a large scymitar was
now directed at my head—or a large pension directed to my pocket—(in the first case at least) I
shou'd speak my mind.

Lord. [*Aside.*] A dangerous young man this!
and I may make something of the discovery.

Twi. [*Aside.*] It tickles him to the soul, I find.
—My Lord, now I begin to be warm on the subject, I feel myself quite agitated—and, from the
intelligence which I have heard, even when I was
in England,—there is every reason to suppose——
exm—exm—exm—[*Mutters.*]

Lord. What, Sir? what?

Twi. You understand me.

Lord. No, Sir—explain.

Twi.

Twi. Why, then, there is every reason to suppose—some people are not what they shou'd be—pardon my thoughts, if they are wrong.

Lord. I *do* pardon your thoughts, with all my heart—but your words, young man, must be answer'd for [*Aside.*] Lady Tremor, good morning.

Twi. [*Aside.*] He is going to ruminate on my sentiments, I dare say.

Lady. Shall we have your Lordship's company towards the evening? Mr. Haswell will be here; if your Lordship has no objection?

Sir Luke. How do you know Mr. Haswell will be here?

Lady. Because he has just called, in his way to the Palace, and said so—and he has been telling us some very interesting stories too.

Sir Luke. Of his morning-visits, I suppose—I heard Meanright say he saw him very busy.

Lady. Sir Luke and I dine out, my Lord; but we shall return early in the evening.

Lord. I will be here, without fail.—Sir Luke, a word with you if you please—[*They come forward.*] Mr. Twineall has taken some very improper liberties with the Sultan's name, and I must insist on making him answer for it.

Sir Luke. My Lord, you are extremely welcome [*Trembling.*] to do whatever your Lordship pleases with any one belonging to me, or to my house—but I hope your Lordship will pay some regard to the master of it.

Lord. O! great regard to the master—and to the mistress also.—But for that gentleman——

Sir Luke. Do *what* your Lordship pleases.

Lord. I will—and I will make him—

Sir Luke. If your Lordship does not forget it.

Lord. I shan't forget it, Sir Luke—I have a very good memory,—when I please.

F 2

Sir

Sir Luke. I don't, in the leaft, doubt it, my Lord
—I never did doubt it.

Lord. And I can be very fevere too, Sir Luke,
when I pleafe.

Sir Luke. I don't, in the leaft, doubt it, my
Lord—I never did doubt it.

Lord. You may depend upon feeing me here in
the evening—and then you fhall find I have not
threatened more than I mean to perform—good
morning!

Sir Luke. Good morning, my Lord—I don't in
the leaft doubt it.   [*Exit Lord* Flint.

Lady. [*Coming forward with* Twineall.] For
Heaven's fake, Mr. Twineall, what has birth to
do with—

Twi. It has to do with *every thing*, Madam—
even with beauty—and I wifh I may fuffer death,
if a woman, with all the mental and perfonal accomplifhments of the fineft creature in Europe,
wou'd to me be of that value, [*Snapping his fingers.*]
if lowly born.

Sir Luke. And I fincerely wifh every man who
vifits me was of the fame opinion.

Aur. For fhame, Mr. Twineall! perfons of mean
birth ought not to be defpifed for what it was not
in their power to prevent—and if it is a misfortune, you fhou'd confider them only as objects of
pity.

Twi. And fo I do pity them—and fo I do—moft
fincerely—poor creatures! [*Looking on Lady* Tremor.

Sir Luke. Aye, now he has mended it finely.

Lady. Mr. Twineall, let me tell you—

Sir Luke. My dear—Lady Tremor— [*Taking
her afide.*] let him alone—let him go on—there is
fomething preparing for him he little expects—fo
let the poor man fay and do what he pleafes, for
the prefent—it won't laft long—for he has offended
                                        my

my Lord Flint; and, I dare say his Lordship will
be able, upon some account or another, to get
him imprisoned for life.

Lady. Imprisoned! Why not take off his head
at once?

Sir Luke. Well, my dear—I am sure I have
no objection—and I dare say my Lord will have it
done, to oblige you.—Egad, I must make friends
with her to keep mine safe.　　　　　[*Aside.*

Lady. Do you mean to take him out to dinner
with us?

Sir Luke. Yes, my dear, if you approve of it—
not else.

Lady. You are grown extremely polite.

Sir Luke. Yes, my dear, his Lordship has taught
me how to be polite.—Mr. Twineall, Lady Tremor and I are going to prepare for our visit, and
I will send a servant to shew you to your apartment, in order to dress, for you will favour us
with your company, I hope?

Twi. Certainly, Sir Luke, I shall do myself
the honour.

Lady. Come this way, Aurelia, I can't bear to
look at him.　　　　　[*Exit with* Aurelia.

Sir Luke. Nor I to *think* of him.　　　[*Exit.*

Twi. If I have not settled my business in this
family, I am mistaken—they seem to have but one
mind about me.—Devilish clever fellow, egad!—
I am the man to send into the world—such a vo-
latile, good-looking scoundrel too! No one sus-
pects me——to be sure I am under some few obligations to my friend for letting me into the different characters of the family—and yet I don't
know whether I am obliged to him or not—for if
he had not made me acquainted with them—I
shou'd soon have had the skill to find them out
myself.—No; I will not think myself under any
　　　　　　　　　　　　　　　obligation

obligation to him—it is devilifh inconvenient for
a gentleman to be under an obligation. [*Exit.*

SCENE II. *The Palace. The Sultan difcovered
with guards and officers attending.*

Hafwell *is conducted in by an officer.*

Sul. Sir, you are fummoned to receive our thanks;
for the troops reftored to health by your kind pre-
fcriptions.—Afk a reward adequate to your fervi-
ces.

Haf. Sultan—the reward I afk, is to preferve
more of your people ftill.

Sul. How more? my fubjects are in health—
no contagion reigns amongft them:

Haf. The prifoner is your fubject—there mifery
— more contagious than difeafe, preys on the
lives of hundreds—fentenced but to confinement,
their doom is death. —Immured in damp and
dreary vaults, they daily perifh—and who can tell
but that amongft the many haplefs fufferers, there
may be hearts, bent down with penitence to Heaven
and you, for every flight offence—there may be
fome amongft the wretched multitude, even inno-
cent victims.—Let me feek them out—let me fave
them, and you.

Sul. Amazement! retract your application—
curb this weak pity; and receive our thanks.

Haf. Curb my pity?—and what can I receive in
recompence for that foft bond, which links me
to the wretched?—and while it fooths their forrow
repays me more, than all the gifts or homage of
an empire.——But if repugnant to your plan of
government—not in the name of pity—but of juftice.

Sul. Juftice!——

Haf.

Haf. The juftice which forbids all but the worft of criminals to be denied that wholefome air the very brute creation freely takes; at leaft allow them *that*.

Sul. Confider, Sir, for whom you plead — for men, (if not bafe culprits) yet fo mifled, fo depraved, they are offenfive to our ftate, and deferve none of its bleffings.

Haf. If not upon the undeferving,—if not upon the haplefs wanderer from the paths of rectitude,— where fhall the fun diffufe his light, or the clouds diftil their dew?. Where fhall fpring breathe fragrance, or autumn pour its plenty?

Sul. Sir, your fentiments, but much more your character, excite my curiofity. They tell me, in our camps, you vifited each fick man's bed,— adminiftered yourfelf the healing draught,—encouraged our favages with the hope of life, or pointed out their *better* hope in death.——The widow fpeaks your charities—the orphan lifps your bounties—and the rough Indian melts in tears to blefs you.——I wifh to afk *why* you have done all this? — What is it prompts you thus to befriend the wretched and forlorn?

Haf. In vain for me to explain — the time it wou'd take to tell you why I act thus——

Sul. Send it in writing then.

Haf. Nay, if you will *read*, I'll fend a book, in which is *already* written why I act thus.

Sul. What book?—What is it called?

Haf. " The Chriftian Doctrine." [Hafwell *bows here with the utmoft reverence.*] There you will find all I have done was but my duty.

Sul. [*To the Guards.*] Retire, and leave me alone with the ftranger. [*All retire except* Hafwell *and the* Sultan. *They come forward.*]

Sul. Your words recall reflections that diftract me;

me; nor can I bear the preffure on my mind without confeffing—I am a Chriftian.

Haf. A Chriftian!—What makes you thus af-fume the apoftate?

Sul. Mifery, and defpair.

Haf. What made you a Chriftian?

Sul. My Arabella,—a lovely European, fent hi-ther in her youth, by her mercenary parents, to fell herfelf to the prince of all thefe territories. But 'twas my happy lot, in humble life, to win her love, fnatch her from his expecting arms, and bear her far away—where, in peaceful foli-tude we lived, till, in the heat of the rebellion againft the late Sultan, I was forced from my happy home to bear a part.—I chofe the imputed rebels fide, and fought for the young afpirer.—An arrow, in the midft of the engagement, pierced his heart; and his officers, alarmed at the terror this ftroke of fate might caufe amongft their troops, urged me (as I bore his likenefs) to coun-terfeit it farther, and fhew myfelf to the foldiers as their king recovered. I yielded to their fuit, becaufe it gave me ample power to avenge the lofs of my Arabella, who had been taken from her home by the mercilefs foe, and barbaroufly murdered.

Haf. Murdered!

Sul. I learnt fo—and my fruitlefs fearch to find her fince has confirmed the intelligence.—Frantic for her lofs, I joyfully embraced a fcheme which promifed vengeance on the enemy—it profpered, —and I revenged my wrongs and her's, with fuch unfparing juftice on the foe, that even the men who made me what I was, trembled to reveal their impofition; and they find it ftill their intereft to continue it.

Haf. Amazement!

Sul.

Sul. Nay, they fill my prifons every day with wretches, that dare whifper I am not the real Sultan, but a ftranger. The fecret, therefore, I myfelf fafely relate in private: the danger is to him who fpeaks it again; and, with this caution, I truft, it is fafe with you.

Haf. It was, without that caution.—Now hear me.——Involved in deeds, in cruelties, which your better thoughts revolt at, the meaneft wretch your camps or prifons hold, claims not half the compaffion *you* have excited. Permit me, then, to be your comforter, as I have been theirs.

Sul. Impoffible!

Haf. In the moft fatal fymptoms I have undertaken the body's cure. The mind's difeafe, perhaps, I'm not lefs a ftranger to — Oh! truft the noble patient to my care.

Sul. How will you begin?

Haf. Lead you to behold the wretched in their mifery, and then fhew you yourfelf in their deliverer.——I have your promife for a boon—'tis this. —Give me the liberty of fix that I fhall name, now in confinement, and be yourfelf a witnefs of their enlargement. — See joy lighted in the countenance where forrow ftill has left its rough remains.—Behold the tear of rapture chafe away that of anguifh — hear the faultering voice, long ufed to lamentation, in broken accents, utter thanks and bleffings.—Behold this fcene, and if you find the medicine ineffectual, difhonour your phyfician.

Sul. I will behold it.

Haf. Come, then, to the governor's houfe this very night—into that council room fo often perverted to the ufe of the torture; and there, unknown to them as their king, you fhall be witnefs

G   to

to all the grateful heart can dictate, and enjoy all that benevolence can taste.

Sul. I will meet you there.

Haf. In the evening?

Sul. At ten precisely. — Guards, conduct the stranger from the palace.   [*Exit Sultan.*

Haf. Thus far advanced, what changes may not be hoped for?   [*Exit,*

END OF THE THIRD ACT.

ACT

A C T   IV.

SCENE I. *An Apartment at Sir* Luke's.

Enter Elvirus *and* Aurelia.

Elvirus.

OH my Aurelia! fince the time I firft faw you—fince you left the pleafant fpot, where I firft beheld you; what diftrefs, what anguifh have we known?

Aur. Your family?

Elv. Yes—and that caufed the filence which I hope you have lamented.—I could not wound you with the recital of our misfortunes—and now, only with the fad idea that I fhall never fee you more, I am come to take my leave.

Aur. Is there a chance that we may never meet again?

Elv. There is—and I hope it too—fincerely hope and requeft it—to fee you again, wou'd be again to behold my father pining in mifery.

Aur. Explain— [*A loud rapping at the door.*] that is, Sir Luke, and Lady Tremor—what fhall I fay, fhou'd they come hither? they fufpect I correfpond with fome perfon in the country—who fhall I fay you are? upon what bufinefs can I fay you are come?

Elv. To avoid all fufpicion of my real fituation, and to be fure to gain admittance, I put on this habit, and told the fervant, when I inquired for you, I was juft arrived from England—[*She ftarts.*] nay, it was but neceffary I fhould conceal who I

was

was in this fuſpicious place, or I might plunge a whole family in the imputed guilt of mine.

Aur. Good Heaven!

Elv. I feared, befides, there was no other means; no likelihood to gain admiſſion—and what, what wou'd I not have ſacrificed, rather than left you for ever without a laſt farewell? think on thefe weighty caufes, and pardon the deception.

Aur. But if they ſhould aſk me—

Elv. Say, as I have done—my ſtay muſt be fo ſhort, it is impoſſible they ſhou'd detect me—for I muſt be back—

Aur. Where?

Elv. No matter where—I muſt be back before the evening—and would almoſt wiſh never to fee you more—I love you, Aurelia—O, how truly! and yet there is a love more dear, more facred ſtill.

Aur. You torture me with ſuſpenſe—Sir Luke is coming this way—what name ſhall I ſay, if he aſks me?

Elv. Glanmore—I announced that name to the fervant.

Aur. You tremble.

Elv. The impoſition hurts me—and I feel as if I dreaded a detection, though 'tis fcarce poſſible —Sorrows have made a coward of me—even the fervant, I thought, looked at me with fuſpicion— and I was both confounded and enraged.

Aur. Go into this apartment; I'll follow you— there we may be fafe—and do not hide the fmalleſt circumſtance which I may have to apprehend.

[*Elvirus exit at a door.*

Sir Luke. [*Without.*] Abominable! provokin! impertinent! not to be borne!

Aur. [*Liſtening.*] Thank Heaven, Sir Luke is ſo perplexed with ſome affairs of his own, he may not think of mine.— [*Exit to* Elvirus.

Enter

Enter Sir Luke, *followed by* Lady Tremor.

Sir Luke. I am out of all patience—and all temper—did you ever hear of fuch a compleat impertinent coxcomb? · Talk, talk, talk, continually! and referring to me on all occafions! " Such " a man was a brave General—another a great " Admiral," and then he muft tell a long ftory about a fiege, and afk me if it did not make my bofom glow!

Lady. It had not that effect upon your face, for you were as white as afhes.

Sir Luke Aye, you did not fee yourfelf, while he was talking of grandfathers and great grandfathers—if you had—

Lady. I was not white, I proteft.

Sir Luke. No—but you were as red as fcarlet.

Lady. And you ought to have refented the infult, if you faw me affected by it—Oh! fome men wou'd have given him fuch a dreffing —

Sir Luke. Yes, my dear, if your uncle the friffeur had been alive, he wou'd have given him a dreffing, I dare fay.

Lady. Sir Luke, none of your impertinence; you know I can't nor won't bear it—neither will I wait for Lord Flint's refentment on Mr. Twineall —No, I defire you will tell him to quit this roof immediately.

Sir Luke. No, my dear—no, no—you muft excufe me—I can't think of quarrelling with a gentleman in my own houfe.

Lady. Was it your own houfe to day at dinner when he infulted us? and would quarrel then?

Sir Luke. No—that was a friend's houfe—and I make it a rule never to quarrel in my own houfe —a friend's houfe—in a tavern—or in the ftreets.

Lady. Well, then, I would quarrel in my own
houfe—

houfe—a friend's houfe—a tavern—or in the ftreets
—if any one offended *me*.

Sir Luke. O, my dear, I have no doubt of it—
no doubt, in the leaft.

Lady. But, at prefent, it fhall be in my own
houfe,—and I will tell the gentleman to quit it
immediately.

Sir Luke. Very well, my dear—pray do.

Lady. I fuppofe, however, I may tell him I
have your authority to bid him go?

Sir Luke. Tell him I have no authority—none
in the world over you—but that you will do as
you like.

Lady. I can't tell him fo—he won't believe it.

Sir Luke. Why not? you often tell me fo, and
make me believe it too.

Lady. Here the gentleman comes—go away
for a moment.

Sir Luke. With all my heart, my dear.

[*Going in a hurry.*

Lady. I'll give him a few hints, that he muft
either change his mode of behaviour, or leave
us.

Sir Luke. That's right—but don't be too warm
—or if he fhould be very impertinent, or infolent—(I hear Aurelia's voice in the next room)
call *her*, and I dare fay fhe'll come and take your
part. [*Exit Sir* Luke.

Enter Twineall.

Twi. I pofitively could pafs a whole day upon
that ftair-cafe—thofe reverend faces!—I prefume
they are the portraits of fome of your Ladyfhip's
illuftrious anceftors.

Lady. Sir! Mr. Twineall—give me leave to
tell you— [*In a violent paffion.*

Twi.

Twi. The word illuftrious, I find, difpleafes you—pardon me—I did not mean to make ufe of fo forcible an epithet—I know the delicacy of fentiment, which cannot bear the reflection that a few centuries only fhou'd reduce from royalty, one, whofe dignified deportment feems to have been formed for that refplendent ftation.

Lady. The man is certainly mad!——Mr. Twineall—

Twi. Pardon me, Madam—I own I am an enthufiaft on thefe occafions—the dignity of blood—

Lady. You have too much, I am fure—do, have a little taken from you.

Twi. Gladly wou'd I lofe every drop that fills thefe plebeian veins, to be enobled by the fmalleft——

Lady. Pray, Sir, take up your abode in fome other place.

Twi. Madam!   [*Surprifed.*

Lady. Your behaviour, Sir—

Twi. If my friend had not given me the hint, damn me if I fhou'd not think her down right angry.   [*Afide.*

Lady. I can fcarce contain my rage at being fo laugh'd at.   [*Afide.*

Twi. I'll mention the wig——this is the time—[*Afide.*] Perhaps you may refent it, Madam—but there is a favour—

Lady. A favour, Sir! is this a time to afk a favour?

Twi. To an admirer of antiquity, as I am.

Lady. Antiquity again!

Twi. I beg pardon——but——a wig, Ma'am—

Lady. A what?   [*Petrified.*

Twi. A wig.   [*Bowing.*

Lady. Oh! oh! oh! [*Choaking.*] this is not to be borne—this is too much—ah! ah! [*Sitting down,*

down, and going into fits.] a direct, plain, palpable, and unequivocal attack upon my family—without evasion or palliative. —I can't bear it any longer.— Oh! oh!—   [*Shrieking.*

Twi. Bless my soul, what shall I do? what's the matter?

Sir Luke. [*Without.*] Maids! maids! go to your mistress—that good-for-nothing fellow is doing her a mischief.

Enter Aurelia.

Aur. Dear Madam, what is the matter?

Enter Sir Luke, *and stands close to the scenes.*

Lady. Oh! oh!   [*Crying.*
Sir Luke. How do you do now, my dear?
Twi. Upon my word, Sir Luke—
Sir Luke. O, Sir, no apology—it does not signify—never mind it—I beg you won't put yourself to the trouble of an apology—it is of no kind of consequence.

Lady. What do you mean, Sir Luke?
                              [*Recovered.*
Sir Luke. To shew proper philosophy, my dear, under the affliction I feel for your distress.

Lady. [*To* Aurelia.] Take Twineall out of the room.

Aur. Mr. Twineall, her Ladyship begs you'll leave the room, till she is a little recovered.

Twi. Certainly. [*Bows respectfully to her Ladyship, and exit with* Aurelia.

Sir Luke. I thought what you wou'd get by quarrelling—fits—and tears.

Lady. And you know, Sir Luke, if you had quarrelled, you wou'd have been in the same situation. [*Rising from her seat.*] But, Sir Luke, my
                                                      dear

dear, Sir Luke, fhow yourfelf a man of courage but on this occafion.—

Sir Luke. My dear, I wou'd do as much for you as I wou'd for my own life—but damn me if I think I could fight to fave that.

Enter Lord Flint.

Lord. Lady Tremor, did the fervant fay you were very well, or very ill?

Lady. Oh, my Lord, that infolent coxcomb, the honourable Mr. Twineall—

Lord. Oh, I am very glad you put me in mind of it—I dare fay I fhou'd have forgot it elfe, notwithftanding I came on purpofe.

Lady. Forgot what?

Lord. A little piece of paper here, [*Pulling out a parchment.*] but it will do a great deal—has he offended you?

Lady. Beyond bearing.

Lord. I am glad of it, becaufe it gives double pleafure to my vengeance—he is a difaffected perfon, Madam—boldly told me he doubted the Sultan's right to the throne—I have informed againft him; and his punifhment is at my option—I may have him imprifoned; fhot; fent to the gallies; or his head cut off—but which does your Ladyfhip chufe?—Which ever you pleafe is at your fervice.
[*Bowing.*

Lady. [*Rifing and curtfying:*] O, they are all alike to me; which ever you pleafe, my Lord.

Sir Luke. What a deal of ceremony!—how cool they are about it.

Lord. And why not cool, Sir; why not cool?

Sir Luke. O, very true—I am fure it has froze me.

Lord. I will go inftantly, for fear it fhou'd

H   flip

flip my memory, and put this paper into the hands of proper officers—in the mean time, Sir Luke, if you can talk with your vifitor, Mr. Twineall, do—inquire his opinion of the Sultan's rights—afk his thoughts, as if you were commiffioned by me—and, while he is revealing them to you, the officers fhall be in ambufh, furprife him in the midft of his fentiments, and bear him away to—

[*Twineall looking in.*

Twi. May I prefume to inquire how your Lady-fhip does ?

Lady. O, yes—and pray walk in—I am quite recovered.

Lord. Lady Tremor, I bid you good day for the prefent.

Sir Luke. [*Following him to the door.*] Your Lord-fhip won't forget ?

Lord. No—depend upon it, I fhall remember.

Sir Luke. Yes—and make fome other people re-member too. [*Exit Lord* Flint.

Twi. Is his Lordfhip gone ? I am very forry.

Sir Luke. No—don't be uneafy, he'll foon be back.

Enter Hafwell.

Sir Luke. Mr. Hafwell, I am glad to fee you.

Haf. I told her Ladyfhip I would call in the evening, Sir Luke ; and fo I have kept my word—I wanted too to fpeak with my Lord Flint, but he was in fuch a hurry as he paffed me, he wou'd hardly let me afk him how he did.—I hope your Ladyfhip is well this afternoon. [*Bows to* Twine-all—*Sir* Luke *exit at the door to* Aurelia *and* Elvirus.

Twi. Pardon me, Mr. Hafwell, but I almoft fufpect you heard of her Ladyfhip's indifpofition,

4 and

and therefore paid this vifit; for I am not to learn your care and attention to all under affliction.

Haf. [*Bows gravely.*] Has your Ladyfhip been indifpofed then?

Lady. A little—but I am much better.

Twi. Surely, of all virtues, charity is the firft! it fo protects our neighbour!

Haf. Do not you think, Sir, *patience* frequently protects him as much?

Twi. Dear Sir—pity for the poor miferable—

Haf. Is oftener excited than the poor and miferable are aware of. [*Looking fignificantly at him.*

Sir Luke. [*From the room where* Aurelia *and* Elvirus *are.*] Nay, Sir, I beg you will walk into this apartment—Aurelia, introduce the gentleman to Lady Tremor.

Lady. Who has fhe with her?

Haf. Aurelia! — O! I have not feen her I know not when—and befides my acquaintance with her relations in England, there is a frank fimplicity about her that—

Enter Sir Luke, *Aurelia, and* Elvirus.

Sir Luke. You fhou'd have introduced the gentleman before—I affure you, Sir, [*To* Elvirus.] I did not know, nor fhou'd I have known, if I had not accidentally come into the room.

Hafwell *ftarts, on feeing* Elvirus.

Sir Luke. [*To Lady* Tremor.] A relation of Aurelia's—a Mr. Glanmore, my dear, juft arrived from England; who call'd to pafs a few minutes with us, before he fets off to the part of India he is to refide in. [Elvirus *and* Aurelia *appear in the utmoft embarraffment and confufion.*

Lady. I hope, Sir, your ftay with us will not be fo fhort as Sir Luke has mentioned?

H 2 *Elv.*

Elv, Pardon me, Madam, it muſt—the cara-
van, with which I travel, goes off this eveniñg,
and I muſt accompany it.

Haſ. [*Aſide.*] I doubted before; but the voice
confirms me.   [*Looking on* Elvirus.

Lady. Why, you only arrived this morning,
did you, Mr. Glanmore? you came paſſenger in
the ſame ſhip, then, with Mr. Twineall?

Twi. No, Madam—Sir, I am very ſorry we
had not the pleaſure of your company on board of
us.   [*To* Elvirus.

Sir Luke. You had;—Mr. Glanmore came over
in the Mercury—did not you tell me ſo, Sir?
                               [Elvirus *bows.*

Twi. Bleſs my ſoul, Sir! I beg your pardon—
but ſurely that cannot be—I got acquainted with
every ſoul on board of us—every creature—all
their connections—and I can ſcarcely ſuppoſe you
were of the number.

Sir Luke. [*Aſide.*] How impertinent he is to
this gentleman too! O! that I had but courage
to knock him down.

Elv. [*To* Twineall.] Perhaps, Sir—

Aur. Yes; I dare ſay, that was the caſe.

Twi. What was the caſe, Madam?

Sir Luke. Wha—wha—wha—[*Mimicks.*] that is
not good breeding.

Haſ. Why do you bluſh, Aurelia?

Aur. Becauſe [*Heſitating.*] this gentleman——
came over in the ſame ſhip with Mr. Twineall.

Sir Luke. And I can't ſay I wonder at your
bluſhing.

Twi. Why then poſitively, Sir, I thought I
had known every paſſenger—and ſurely—

Lady. Mr. Twineall, your behaviour puts me
out of all patience—did you not hear the gentle-
                                          man

man fay he came in the fame veffel; and is not that fufficient?

Twi. Perfectly, Madam — perfectly — but I thought there might be fome miftake.

Elv. And there is, Sir—you find you are miftaken.

Lady. I thought fo.——

Haf. [*To* Elvirus.] And you *did* come in the fame veffel?

Elv. Sir, do *you* doubt it?

Haf. Doubt it?

Elv. Dare not doubt it. —[*Trembling and confufed.*

Haf. Dare not?

Elv. No, Sir, dare not.   [*Violently.*

Aur. Oh, heavens!

Sir Luke. [*To* Aurelia.] Come, my dear, you and I will get out of the way. [*Retiring with her.*

Lady. O, dear! — for heaven's fake! — Mr. Twineall, this is your doing.

Twi. Me, Madam!——

Haf. I beg the company's pardon—but [*To* Elvirus.] a fingle word with you, Sir, if you pleafe.

Lady. Dear Mr. Hafwell——

Haf. Truft my prudence and forbearance, Madam — I will but fpeak a word in private to this gentleman. — [*Hafwell takes* Elvirus *down to the bottom of the ftage; the reft retire.*

Haf. Are you, or are you not, an impoftor?

Elv. I am—I am—but do not you repeat my words—Do not *you* fay it.   [*Threatening.*

Haf. What am I to fear?

Elv. Fear *me*—I cannot lie with fortitude; but I can——Beware of me. .

Haf. I *will* beware of you, and fo fhall all my friends.

Elv.

Elv. Infolent, infulting man.—[*With the utmoft contempt.*

Lady Tremor *and the reft come down.*

Lady. Come, come, gentlemen, I hope you are now perfectly fatisfied about this little non-fenfe.—Let us change the fubject.—Mr. Hafwell, have you been fuccefsful before the Sultan for any of thofe poor prifoners you vifited this morning?

Sir Luke. Aye; Meanright told me he faw you coming from them with your long cloak; and faid he fhou'd not have known you, if fomebody had not faid it was you.

[Elvirus *looks with furprife, confufion, and repen-tance.*]

Lady. But what fuccefs with the Sultan?

Haf. He has granted me the pardon and free-dom of any fix I fhall prefent as objects of his mercy.

Lady. I fincerely rejoice.—Then the youth and his father, whom you felt fo much for, I am fure, will be in the number of thofe who fhare your clemency.

[Hafwell *makes no reply, and after a paufe*]—

Elv. [*With the moft fupplicatory tone and manner.*] Sir—Mr. Hafwell—O, heavens!

Sir Luke. Come, Mr. Hafwell, this young man feems forry he has offended you—forgive him.

Lady. Aye, do, Mr. Hafwell — are you forry, Sir?

Elv. O! wounded to the heart—and, without his pardon, fee nothing but defpair.

Lady. Good heavens!

Haf. Sir Luke, my Lord Flint told me he was coming back directly—pray inform him I had bufinefs elfewhere, and cou'd wait no longer.

[*Exit.*

Elv.

Elv. O! I'm undone.

Lady. Follow him, if you have any thing to fay?

Elv. I *dare* not—I feel the terror of his juft reproach.

Lady. Did you know him in England?

Aur. Dear Madam, will you fuffer me to fpeak a few words—— [*Afide to Lady* Tremor.

Sir Luke. Aye; leave her and her relation together, and let us take a turn in the garden with Mr. Twineall.—I'm afraid his Lordfhip will be back before we have drawn him to fay more on the fubject, for which he will be arrefted.

Lady. You are right.

Sir Luke. Mr. Twineall, will you walk this way? — That young lady and gentleman wifh to have a little converfation.

Twi. O, certainly, Sir Luke, by all means. [*Exeunt Sir* Luke *and Lady.*

[*To* Elvirus.] I am extremely forry, Sir, you kept your bed during the voyage: I fhou'd elfe have been moft prodigioufly happy in fuch good company. [*Exit.*

Aur. Why are you thus agitated? It was wrong to be fo impetuous—but fuch regret as this——

Elv. Hear the fecret I refufed before—my father is a prifoner for life.

Aur. Oh, heavens! then Mr. Hafwell was the only man——

Elv. And he had promifed me — promifed me, with benevolence, his patronage — but the difguife he wore when I firft faw him, led me to miftake him now—made me expofe my falfehood, my infamy, and treat his honour'd perfon with abufe.

Aur. Aye; let his virtues make you thus repent;

pent; but let them alfo make you hope forgivenefs.

Elv. Nay, he is juft, as well as compaffionate—
and for detected falfehood ——

Aur. You make me tremble.

Elv. Yet he fhall hear my ftory—I'll follow
him, and obtain his pity, if not his pardon.

Aur. Nay, fupplicate for that too — and you
need not blufh, or feel yourfelf degraded, to *kneel*
to HIM, for he wou'd fcorn the pride that tri-
umphs over the humbled.   *[Exeunt.*

SCENE II.   *The Garden.*

Enter Sir Luke, Twineall, *and Lady* Tremor.

Twi. Why, really, Sir Luke, as my Lord has
given you charge to found my principles, I muft
own they are juft fuch as I delivered to him.

Sir Luke. Well, Mr. Twineall, I only wifh you
to be a little more clear—we will fuppofe the prefent Sultan no impoftor—yet what pretenfions do
you think the *other* family——

Twi. That I'll make clear to you at once — or
if my reafons are *not* very clear, they are at leaft
very *pofitive,* and that you know is the fame
thing.—This family—no—that family—the family that reigned before this—this came after
that—they came before. Now every one agrees
that this family was always—fo and fo—[*whifpering.*]—and that the other was always—fo and fo—
[*whifpering.*] — in fhort, every body knows that
one of them had always a very fufpicious—you
know what——

Sir Luke. No, I don't.

Twi. Pfhaw—pfhaw—every body conjectures
what—and though it was never faid in fo many
                                              words,

words, yet it was always fuppofed — and though there never has been any proof, yet there have been things much more ftrong—and for that very reafon, Sir William—(Sir Luke, I mean—I beg your pardon)—for that very reafon — (I can't think what made me call you Sir William)—*for that very reafon* — (Oh, I was thinking of Sir William Tiffany)—for that very reafon, fay people what they will—*that, that* muft be their opinion—but then where is the man who will fpeak his thoughts freely as I have done ?

Enter Guards, who had been liftening at a diftance during this fpeech.

Sir Luke. [*Starting.*] Blefs my foul, gentlemen, you made my heart jump to my very lips.

Guard. [*To* Twineall.] Sir, you are our prifoner, and muft go with us.

Twi. Gentlemen, you are miftaken—I had all my clothes made in England, and 'tis impoffible the bill can have followed me already.

Guard. Your charge, is fomething againft the ftate.

Twi. Againft the ftate ?—You are miftaken—it cannot be me.

Guard. No—there is no miftake.—[*Pulling out a paper.*]—You are here called Henry Twineall.

Twi. But if they have left out *honourable*, it can't be me —— I am the Honourable Henry Twineall.

Sir Luke. Aye, that you are to prove before your judges.

Guard. Yes, Sir—and we are witneffes of the long fpeech you have juft now been making.

Twi. And pray, gentlemen, did you know what I meant by it ?

I

Guard. Certainly.

Twi. Why, then, upon my foul, it was more than I did—I wifh I may be facrificed ——

Sir Luke. Well, well, you are *going* to be facrificed—Don't be impatient.

Twi. But, gentlemen—Sir Luke !

[*The Guards feize him.*

Lady, Dear Mr. Twineall, I am afraid you will have occafion for the dignity of all my anceftors to fupport you under this trial.

Sir Luke. And have occafion for all my courage too.

Twi. But, Sir—but, gentlemen——

Sir Luke. Oh ! I wou'd not be in your coat, fafhionable as it is, for all the Sultan's dominions.

[*Exit Sir* Luke *and Lady*—Twineall, *and* Guards—*feparately.*

END OF THE FOURTH ACT.

ACT V.

SCENE I. *The Prison.*

Haſwell *and the female Priſoner diſcovered.*

Haſwell.

RATHER remain in this loathſome priſon!—
refuſe the bleſſing offered you!—the bleſſing your
pleaſed fancy formed ſo precious you durſt not
even truſt its reality!

Priſ. No—while my pleaſed *fancy* only ſaw the
proſpect, I own it was delightful; but now rea-
ſon beholds it within my reach, the view is
changed—and what, in the gay dream of fond de-
lirium, ſeemed a bleſſing, in my waking hours of
ſad reflection would prove the moſt ſevere of pu-
niſhments.

Haſ. Explain—what is the cauſe that makes
you think thus?

Priſ. A cauſe that has alone for fourteen years
made me reſigned to a fate like this.—When you
firſt mentioned my releaſe from this drear place,
my wild ideas included, with the light, all that had
ever made the light a bleſſing—'twas not the *ſun*
I ſaw in my mad tranſport, but a loſt huſband
filled my roving fancy—'twas his idea that gave
the colours of the world their beauty, and made
me fondly hope to graſp its ſweets.

Haſ. A huſband!

Priſ. But the world that I was wont to enjoy

I 2   with

with him—to fee again without him—every well-known object would wound my mind with dear remembrances for ever loft, and make my freedom torture.

Haf. But yet——

Prif. Oh! on my knees a thoufand times I have thanked Heaven that *he* partook not of this dire abode—that he fhared not with me my hard ufage! —a greater blefling I poffefs'd from that, than all his loved fociety cou'd have given — but in a happy world, where fmiling nature pours her boundlefs gifts!—oh! there his lofs wou'd be unfufferable.

Haf. Do you lament him dead?

Prif. Yes—or, like me, a prifoner—elfe he wou'd have fought me out—have fought his Arabella!—[Hafwell *ftarts.*]—Why do you ftart?

Haf. Are you a Chriftian?—an European?

Ara. I am.

Haf. The name made me fuppofe it.—I am fhocked that——the Chriftian's fufferings—[*Trying to conceal his furprife.*]—but were you made a prifoner in the *prefent* Sultan's reign?

Ara. Yes, or I had been fet free on his afcent to the throne; for he gave pardon to all the enemies of the flain monarch : but I was taken in a veffel, where I was hurried in the heat of the battle with a party of the late Emperor's friends —and all the prifoners were by the officers of the prefent Sultan fent to flavery, or confined, as I have been, in hopes of ranfom from their friends.

Haf. And did never intelligence or inquiry reach you from your hufband?

Ara. Never.

Haf. Never?

Ara. I once was informed of a large reward for the difcovery of a female Chriftian, and, with

boundlefs

boundlefs hopes, afked an interview with the meffenger; but found, on inquiry, *I* could not anfwer his defcription, as he *fecretly* informed me it
was the Sultan who made the fearch for one *he*
himfelf had known and dearly loved.

Haf. Good Heaven!—[*Afide.*]—You then conclude your hufband dead?

Ara. I do;—or, like me, by fome mifchance,
taken with the other party, and having no friend
to plead his caufe before the Emperor, whom he
ferved——

Haf. I'll plead it—fhould I ever chance to find
him—but, ere we can hope for other kindnefs, you
muft appear before the Sultan — thank him for
the favour which you now decline, and tell the
caufe why you cannot accept it.

Ara. Alas! almoft worn out with forrow — an
object of affliction as I am—in pity, excufe me—
prefent my thanks—my humble gratitude—but
pardon my attendance.

Haf. Nay, you muft go — it is neceffary — I
will accompany you to him. — Retire a moment;
but when I fend, be ready.

Ara. I fhall obey. [*She bows obediently, and exit.*
[*As* Hafwell *comes down,* Elvirus *places
himfelf in his path*—Hafwell *ftops, looks
at him with an auftere earneftnefs, which*
Elvirus *obferving, turns away his face.*

Elv. Nay, reproach me — I can bear your an-
ger, but do not let me meet your eye—Oh! it is
more awful, now I know who you are, than if
you had kingdoms to difperfe, or could deal in-
ftant death.—[Hafwell *looks on him with a manly
firmnefs, then walks on,* Elvirus *following him.*]—
I do not plead for my father now. — Since what
has paffed, I only afk forgivenefs.

Haf.

Haf. Do you forgive yourself?
Elv. I never will.

Enter Keeper.

Keep. One of our prisoners, who, in his cell, makes the most pitious moans, has sent to entreat that Mr. Haswell will not leave this place till he has heard his complaints and supplications.

Haf. Bring me to him.   [*Going.*

Elv. Nay, leave me not thus — perhaps never to see you more!——

Haf. You shall see me again—in the mean time, reflect on what you merit.   [*Exit with* Keeper.

Elv. And what is that?—Confusion!—and yet, he says, I am to see him again—speak with him. —Oh! there's a blessing to the most abandoned, a divine propensity (they know not why) to commune with the virtuous!   [*Exit.*

SCENE II.   *The first Prison Scene.*

Enter second Keeper, Haswell *following.*

Haf. Where is the poor unfortunate?

2d Keep. Here, Sir.

Haf. Am I to behold greater misery still? — a still greater object of compassion?

[*Second* Keeper *opens a door, and* Twineall *enters a prisoner, in one of the prison dresses.*

Haf. What have we here?

Twi. Don't you know me, Mr. Haswell?

Haf. I beg your pardon, Sir— I beg your pardon—but is it?—is it?——

Twi. Why, Mr. Haswell—if you don't know me, or won't know me, I shall certainly lose my senses.

                                             Haf.

Haf. O, I know you—know you very well.

Twi. What, notwithstanding the alteration in my dress?—there was a hard thing!

Haf. O, I'll procure you that again —and, for all things else, I'm sure you will have patience.

Twi. O, no, I can't—upon my soul I can't.— I want a little lavender water—My hair is in such a trim too!—No powder—no brushes——

Haf. I will provide you with them all.

Twi. But who will you provide to look at me, when I am dress'd?

Haf. I'll bring all your acquaintance.

Twi. I had rather you wou'd take me to see them.

Haf. Pardon me.

Twi. Dear Mr. Hafwell!— Dear Sir!— Dear friend!—What shall I call you?— Only say what title you like best, and I'll call you by it directly — I always did love to please every body— and I am sure at this time I stand more in need of a friend than ever I did in my life.

Haf. What has brought you here?

Twi. Trying to get a place.

Haf. A place?

Twi. Yes; and you see I have got one — and a poor place it is! — in short, Sir, my crime is said to be an offence against the state; and they tell me no friend on earth but you can get that re- mitted.

Haf. Upon my word, the pardons I have ob- tained are for so few persons—and those already promised——

Twi. O, I know I am no favourite of yours— you think me an impertinent, silly, troublesome fellow, and that my conduct in life will be nei- ther of use to my country nor of benefit to so- ciety.

Haf.

Haf. You miftake me, Sir—I think fuch gla-
ring imperfections as yours will not be of fo
much difadvantage to fociety as thofe of a lefs-
faulty man.—In beholding your conduct, thou-
fands fhall turn from the paths of folly, to which
fafhion, cuftom, nature, (or call it what you will)
impels them ;—therefore, Mr. Twineall, if not
pity for your faults, yet a concern for the good
effect they may have upon the world (fhou'd you
be admitted there again) will urge me to folicit
your return to it.

Twi. Sir, you have fuch powers of oratory —
what a prodigious capital quality ! — and I doubt
not but you are admired by the world equally for
that——

Enter Meffenger *to* Hafwell.

Meff. Sir, the Sultan is arrived in the council
chamber, and has fent me.   [*Whifpers.*

Haf. I come.—Mr. Twineall, farewell for the
prefent.   [*Exit with* Meffenger.

Twi. Now, what was that whifper about ?—
Oh, heavens ! perhaps my death in agitation.—
I have brought myfelf into a fine fituation ! —
done it by wheedling too !

2d Keep. Come, your bufinefs with Mr. Hafwell being ended, return to your cell. [*Roughly.*

Twi. Certainly, Sir — certainly ! — O, yes ! —
How happy is this prifon in having fuch a keeper
as you !—fo mild, fo gentle—there is fomething
about you,—I faid, and I thought the moment I
had the *happinefs* of meeting you here, — Dear
me !—what wou'd one give for fuch a gentleman
as him in England ! — You wou'd be of infinite
fervice to fome of our young bucks, Sir.

                                        2d Keep.

2d Keep. Go to your cell — go to your cell.
[*Roughly.*

Twi. This world wou'd be nothing without elegant manners, and elegant people in all ftations of
life.—[*Enter* Meffenger, *who whifpers fecond* Keeper.]—Another whifper !   [*Terrified.*

2d Keep. No ; come this way. — The judge is
now fitting in the hall, and you muft come before
him.

Twi. Before the judge, Sir — O, dear Sir ! —
what, in this defhabille ? — in this coat ? — Dear
me !—but to be fure one muft conform to cuftoms
— to the cuftom of the country where one is. —
[*He goes to the door, and then ftops.*] — I beg your
pardon, Sir—wou'd not you chufe to go firft ?

2d Keep. No.
Twi. O !   [*Exeunt.*

SCENE III.   *The Council Chamber.*

Enter Sultan, Hafwell, *aud* Guards.

Haf. Sultan, I have out-run your bounty in my
promifes ; and one poor, unhappy female——

Sul. No — you named yourfelf the number to
releafe, and it is fixed—I'll not increafe it.

Haf. A poor, miferable female——

Sul. Am I lefs miferable than fhe is ?—And who
fhall releafe me from my forrows ?

Haf. Then let me tell you, Sultan, fhe is above
your power to oblige, or to punifh. — Ten years,
nay more, confinement in a drear cell has been no
greater punifhment to her, than had fhe lived in a
pleafant world without the man fhe loved.

Sul. Hah !

Haf. And freedom offered fhe rejects with fcorn,
becaufe he is not included in the bleffing.

K   *Sul.*

Sul. You talk of prodigies!—[*He makes a sign for the Guards to retire, and they exit.*]—and yet I once knew a heart equal to this description.

Haf. Nay, will you see her?—Witness yourself the fact?

Sul. Why do I tremble?—My busy fancy presents an image——

Haf. Yes, tremble, indeed!   [*Threatening.*

Sul. Hah! have a care—what tortures are you preparing for me?—My mind shrinks at the idea.

Haf. Your wife you will behold—whom you have kept in want, in wretchedness, in a damp dungeon, for these fourteen years, because you wou'd not listen to the voice of pity.——Dread her look—her frown—not for herself alone, but for hundreds of her fellow sufferers—and while your selfish fancy was searching, with wild anxiety, for her *you* loved, unpitying, you forgot others might love like you.

Sul. O! do not bring me to a trial which I have not courage to support.

Haf. She attends without—I sent for her to thank you for the favour she declines.—Nay, be composed—she knows *you* not—cannot, thus disguised as the Sultan.   [*Exit* Hafwell.

Sul. Oh! my Arabella! could I have thought that your approach wou'd ever impress my mind with horror!—or that, instead of flying to your arms with all the love I bear you, terror and dread shou'd fix me a statue of remorse.

Enter Hafwell, *leading* Arabella.

Haf. Here kneel, and return your thanks.

Sul. My Arabella! worn with grief and anguish!   [*Aside.*

Ara. [*Kneeling to the* Sultan.] Sultan, the favour
vour

vour you wou'd beſtow, I own, and humbly thank you for.

Sul. Gracious Heaven!   [*In much agitation.*

Ara. But as I am now accuſtomed to confinement, and the idea of all the world can give, cannot inſpire a wiſh that warms my heart to the enjoyment—I ſupplicate permiſſion to transfer the bleſſing you have offered, to one of thoſe who may have friends to welcome their return from bondage, and ſo make freedom precious. — I have none to rejoice at *my* releaſe — none to lament my deſtiny while a priſoner.—And were I free, in this vaſt world (forlorn and friendleſs) 'tis but a priſon ſtill.

Sul. What have I done?—[*Throwing himſelf on a ſopha with the greateſt emotion.*

Haſ. Speak to him again. — He repents of the ſeverity with which he has cauſed his fellow creatures to be uſed.—Tell him *you* forgive him.

Ara. [*Going to him.*] Believe me, Emperor, I forgive all who have ever wronged me — all who have ever cauſed my ſufferings. — Pardon *you!* — Alas! I have pardoned even thoſe who tore me from my huſband!—Oh, Sultan! all the tortures you have made me ſuffer, compared to ſuch a pang as that—did I ſay I had forgiven it?—Oh! I am afraid—afraid I have not yet.

Sul. Forgive it now, then, for he is reſtored. —[*Taking off his turban.*]— Behold him in the Sultan, and once more ſeal his pardon.—[*She faints on* Haſwell.]—Nay, pronounce it quickly, or my remorſe for what you have undergone, will make my preſent tortures greater than any my cruelties have ever yet inflicted.

Ara. [*Recovering.*] Is this the light you promiſed?—[*To* Haſwell.]— Dear precious light!— Is this my freedom? to which I bind myſelf a

ſlave

flave for ever. — [*Embracing the* Sultan.]—Was I *your* captive ?—Sweet captivity !—more precious than an age of liberty !

Sul. Oh, my Arabella ! through the amazing changes of my fate, (which I will foon difclofe) think not but I have fearched for *thee* with unceafing care ; but the blefling to behold you once again was left for my kind monitor alone to beftow. —— Oh, Hafwell ! had I, like you, made others' miferies my concern, like you fought out the wretched, how many days of forrow had I fpared myfelf as well as others — for I long fince had found my Arabella.

Ara. Oh, Heaven ! that weigheft our fufferings with our joys, and as our lives decline feeft in the balance thy bleffings far more ponderous than thy judgements—be witnefs, I complain no more of what I have endured, but find an ample recompence this moment.

Haf. I told you, Sir, how you might be happy.

Sul. ——Take your reward—(to a heart like yours, more valuable than treafure from my coffers) — this fignet, with power to redrefs the *wrongs* of all who fuffer.

Haf. Valuable indeed !—

Ara. [*To* Hafwell.] Oh, virtuous man !—to reward *thee* are we made happy—to give thy pitying bofom the joy to fee us fo, has Heaven remitted its intended punifhment of continued feparation.

Sul. Come, my beloved wife ! — come to my palace — there, equally, my deareft blefling, as when the cottage gave its fewer joys—and in him [*To* Hafwell.] we not only find our prefent happinefs, but dwell fecurely on our future hopes—for here, I vow, before he leaves our fhores, I will adopt every meafure he fhall point out—and that period of my life whereon he fhall lay his cenfure,

that

that will I fix apart for penitence. — [*Exit* Sultan
and Arabella. — Haſwell *bows to Heaven with
thanks.*

Enter Keeper.

Keep. An Engliſh priſoner, juſt now condemned
to loſe his head, one Henry Twineall, humbly
begs permiſſion to ſpeak a few ſhort ſentences, his
laſt dying words, to Mr. Haſwell.

Haſ. Condemned to loſe his head? — Lead me
to him.

Keep. O, Sir, you need not hurry yourſelf—it
is off by this time, I dare ſay.

Haſ. Off?

Keep. Yes, Sir — we don't ſtand long about
theſe things in this country—I dare ſay it is off.

Haſ. [*Impatiently.*] Lead me to him inſtantly.

Guard. O! 'tis of conſequence, is it, Sir?—
if that is the caſe——

[*Exit* Keeper, *followed by* Haſwell.

SCENE IV. *An arch-way at the top of the ſtage,
through which ſeveral Guards enter* —Twineall
*in the middle, dreſſed for execution, with a large
book in his hand.*

Twi. One more verſe, gentlemen, if you pleaſe.

Off. The time is expired.

Twi. One more, gentlemen, if you pleaſe.

Off. The time is expired.

Enter Haſwell.

Twi. Oh! my dear Mr. Haſwell!

[*Burſting into tears.*

Haſ.

Haf. What, in tears at parting with me?—
This is a compliment indeed!

Twi. I hope you take it as such — I am sure I
mean it as such. — It kills me to leave *you* — it
breaks my heart;—and I once flattered myself
such a charitable, good, feeling, humane heart as
you possess——

Haf. Hold! Hold! — This, Mr. Twineall, is
the vice which has driven you to the fatal precipice
whereon you are—and in death will you not relin-
quish it?

Twi. What vice, Sir, do you mean?

Haf. Flattery! — a vice that renders you not
only despicable, but odious.

Twi. But how has flattery been the cause?

Haf. Your English friend, before he left the
island, told me what information you had asked
from him, and that he had given you the direct
opposite of every person's character, as a just pu-
nishment for your mean premeditation and de-
signs.

Twi. I never imagined that amiable friend had
sense enough to impose upon any body!

Haf. Yet I presume, he could not suppose fate
wou'd have carried their resentment to a length
like this.

Twi. Oh! cou'd fate be arrested in its course!

Haf. You wou'd reform your conduct?

Twi. I wou'd—I wou'd never say another civil
thing to any body — never — never make myself
agreeable again.

Haf. Release him—here is the Sultan's sig-
net.   [*They release him.*

Twi. Oh! my dear Mr. Haswell! never was
compassion!—never benevolence!—never such a
heart as yours!——

Haf.

Haf. Sieze him—he has broken his contract
already.

Twi. No, Sir—No, Sir—I protest you are an
illnatured, furly, crabbed fellow. I always thought
so, upon my word, whatever I have said.

Haf. And, I'll forgive *that* meaning, sooner
than the other—utter any thing but flattery—
Oh ! never let the honest, plain, *blunt* English
name, become a proverb for so bafe a vice.——

Lady. Ter. [*Without.*] Where is the poor creature ?

Enter Lady Tremor.

Lady. Oh ! if his head is off, pray let me
look at it ?——

Twi. No, Madam, it is on—and I am very
happy to be able to tell you fo.——

Lady. Dear Heaven !—I expected to have feen
it off !—but no matter—as it is on—I am come
that it may be kept on—and have brought my
Lord Flint, and Sir Luke, as witneffes.

Enter Lord, Aurelia, *and* Sir Luke.

Haf. Well, Madam, and what have they to fay?

Sir Luke. Who are we to tell our ftory to ?—
There does not feem to be any one fitting in judgement.—

Haf. Tell it to me, Sir—I will report it.

Sir Luke. Why then, Mr. Hafwell, as Ghofts
fometimes walk—and as one's confcience is fometimes troublefome—I think Mr. Twineall has
done nothing to merit death, and the charge
which his Lordfhip fent in againft him, we begin
to think too fevere—but, if there was any falfe
ftatement——

Lord. It was the fault of my not charging my
memory

memory—any error I have been guilty of, muſt be laid to the fault of my total want of memory.

Haſ. And what do you hope from this confeſſion?

Sir Luke. To remit the priſoner's puniſhment of death to ſomething leſs, if the Sultan will pleaſe to annul the ſentence

Lord. Yes—and grant ten or twelve years impriſonment—or the Gallies for fourteen years — or——

Sir Luke. Ay, ay, ſomething in that way.

Haſ. For ſhame—for ſhame—Gentlemen!— the extreme rigour you ſhew in puniſhing a diſſenſion from your opinion, or a ſatire upon your folly, proves to conviction, what reward you had beſtowed upon the *ſkilful* flatterer.

Twi. Gentlemen and Ladies, pray why wou'd you wiſh me requited with ſuch extreme ſeverity, merely for my humble endeavours to make myſelf agreeable?—Lady Tremor, upon my honour I was credibly informed, your anceſtors were Kings of Scotland.

Lady. Impoſſible!—you might as well ſay that you heard Sir Luke had diſtinguiſhed himſelf at the battle of——

Twi. And, I *did* hear ſo.

Lady. And he *did* diſtinguiſh himſelf; for he was the only one that ran away.

Twi. Cou'd it happen?

Lady. Yes, Sir, it did happen.

Sir Luke. And go *you*, Mr. Twineall, into a field of battle, and I think it is very likely to happen again.

Lord. If Mr. Haſwell has obtained your pardon, Sir, it is all very well—but let me adviſe you to keep your ſentiments on politics to yourſelf,

felf, for the future—as you value that pretty head of yours.

Twi. I thank you, Sir—I do value it.

Enter Elvirus.

Haf. [*Going to him.*] Aurelia, in this letter to me, has explained your ftory with fo much com-paffion, that, for her fake, I muft pity it too.—With freedom to your father, and youfelf, the Sultan reftore's his forfeited lands—and might I plead, Sir Luke, for your intereft with Aureila's friends, this youug man's filial love, fhou'd be repaid by conjugal affection.

Sir Luke. As for that, Mr. Hafwell, you have fo much intereft at court, that your taking the young man under you protection——befides, as Aurelia was fent hither merely to get a hufband—I don't fee——

Aur. True, Sir Luke—and I am afraid my father and mother will begin to be uneafy that I have not got one yet—and I fhou'd be very forry to difoblige them.

Elv. No—fay rather, forry to make me wretch-ed.— [*Taking her hand.*

Enter Zedan.

Haf. My Indian friend, have you received your freedom ?

Zed. Yes—and come to bid you farewell—which I wou'd *never* do, had I not a family in wretchednefs till my return—for you fhou'd be my mafter, and I *wou'd* be your flave.——

Haf. I thank you—may you meet at home eve-ry comfort !

Zed. May you—may you—what fhall I fay ?
L May

—May you once in your life be a prifoner—then releafed—to feel fuch joy, as I feel now!——

Haf. I thank you for a wifh, that tells me moft emphatically, how much you think I have ferved you.

Twi. And, my dear Lord, I fincerely wifh you may once in your life, have your head chopped off—juft to know what I fhou'd have felt, in that fituation.——

Zed. [*Pointing to* Hafwell.] Are all his country-men as good as he ?

Sir Luke. No-no-no-no—not *all*—but the worft of them are good enough to admire him.

Twi. Pray Mr. Hafwell, will you fuffer all thefe encomiums ?

Elv. He *muft* fuffer them—there are virtues, which praife cannot taint—fuch are Mr. Hafwell's —for they are the offspring of a mind, fuperior even to the love of fame—neither can they, through malice, fuffer by applaufe, fince they are too facred to incite envy, and muft conciliate the refpect, the love, and the admiration of all.

F I N I S.

E P I L O G U E,

Written by MILES-PETER ANDREWS, Efq.

Spoken by Mrs. MATTOCKS.

SINCE all are fprung, they fay, from Mother Earth,
Why ftamp a merit or difgrace on birth?
Yet fo it is, however we difguife it,
All boaft their origin, or elfe defpife it.
This pride or fhame haunts ev'ry living foul·
From Hyde-park Corner, down to Limehoufe Hole:
Peers, taylors, poets, ftatefmen, undertakers,
Knights, fquires, man-milliners, and peruke-makers.
Sir Hugh Glengluthglin, from the land of goats,
Tho' out at elbows, fhews you all his coats;
And rightful heir to *twenty pounds* per annum,
Boafts the rich blood that warm'd his great great gran-
    nam;
While wealthy Simon Soapfuds; juft be·knighted,
Struck with the fword of ftate, is grown dim fighted,
Forgets the neighbouring chins he ufed to lather,
And fcarcely knows he ever had a father.

  Our Author, then, correct in every line,
From nature's characters hath pictur'd mine;
For many a lofty fair, who, friz'd and curl'd,
With creft of horfe hair, tow'ring thro' the world,
To powder, pafte, and pins, ungrateful grown,
Thinks the full periwig is all her own;
Proud of her conquering ringlets, onward goes,
Nor thanks the barber, from whofe hands fhe rofe:

  Thus doth falfe pride fantaftic minds miflead,
And make our weaker fex feem weak indeed:
Suppofe, to prove this truth, in mirthful ftrain,
We bring the *Dripping family* again.——
Papa, a tallow chandler by defcent,
Had read " how *larning* is moft excellent:"
So Mifs, returned from boarding fchool at Bow,
Waits to be finifhed by Mama and Co.——

" See,

EPILOGUE.

" *See, spouse, how spruce our Nan is grown, and tall;*
" *I'll lay, she cuts a dash at Lord Mayor's ball.*"—
In bolts the maid—" *Ma'am! Miss's master's come;*"—
Away fly Ma' and Miss to dancing room—
" *Walk in, Mounseer; come, Nan, draw up like me.*"—
" *Ma foi! Madame, Miss like you as two pea.*"—
Mounseer takes out his kit; the scene begins;
Miss trusses up; my lady Mother grins;—
" *Ma'amselle, me teach a you de step to tread;*
" *First turn you toe, den turn you littel head;*
" *One, two, dree, sinka, risa, balance; bon,*
" *Now entrechat, and now de cotillon.*
                              [*Singing and dancing about.*
" *Pardieu, Ma'amselle be one enchanting girl;*
" *Me no surprise to see her ved an Earl.*"—
' *'With all my heart, says Miss; Mounseer, I'm ready;*
" *I dream'd last night, Ma, I should be a Lady.*"

   Thus do the *Drippings*, all important grown,
Expect to shine with lustre not their own;
New airs are got; fresh graces, and fresh washes,
New caps, new gauze, new feathers, and new sashes;
Till just complete for conquest at Guildhall,
Down comes an order to suspend the ball.
Miss Shrieks, Ma' scolds, Pa' seems to have lost his
         tether;
Caps, custards, coronets—all sink together—
Papa resumes his jacket, dips away,
And Miss lives single, till next Lord Mayor's day.

   If such the *sorrow*, and if such the strife,
That break the comforts of domestic life,
Look to the hero, who this night appears,
Whose boundless excellence the World reveres;
Who, friend to nature, by no blood confin'd,
Is the glad relative of all mankind.

CPSIA information can be obtained
at www.ICGtesting.com
Printed in the USA
LVHW051610251122
733960LV00003B/492